Human Capital: The Untapped Treasure

Human Capital:
The Untapped Treasure

by

Gerald G. Polesky, Ph.D.

DBM Press LC
6412 Brandon Ave, #123
Springfield, VA 22150

First published in 2009 by

DBM Press, LC
6412 Brandon Ave, #123
Springfield, VA 22150
dbmpress@yahoo.com

See our catalogue at http://www.dbmpress.com

For quality used and rare books, see our catalogues at:
http://www.dbookmahn.com

Library of Congress Control Number: 2009931911

ISBN-10: 0-9816102-2-6
ISBN-13: 978-0-9816102-2-1

First Edition

1st Printing
10 9 8 7 6 5 4 3 2 1

Printed in the United States of America

Produced for the publisher by
BRIOprint, 12 S. Sixth Street, #1020, Minneapolis, MN 55402

Dedication

I am dedicating this book
to my daughters
Larissa
who brought pleasure to so many;
Tiffany
who may be one of the few people
who understands true friendship,
and to my wife Madeline,
for her unconditional love and support

Human Capital: The Untapped Treasure

Contents

Acknowledgments

The most enjoyable aspect of writing *Human Capital: the Untapped Treasure* is possibly acknowledging everyone who has contributed to it. Although this book lists one author, more than anything else the book is a compilation of the information borrowed from many individuals who added to my learning by placing their ideas on paper. I am grateful to my colleagues, mentors, teachers and students who have unknowingly supplemented my understanding. I am particularly thankful for my friend John Gumpert, who as a mentor stimulated me through his intellectual sharing, questioning and encouragement, inspiring me to deeper thought.

I have also been fortunate to have the opportunity to meet and interact with many business colleagues from whom I have learned a great deal. Dr. W. Edwards Deming's philosophy of *profound knowledge* started me on a never-ending journey of continual learning and the assimilation of worker's awareness. Debra Amidon who became a *pathfinder* in my pursuit of education helped me understand the importance for the need to collaborate and share. Then there is Elizabeth Bluemke of the Society of Management Accountants of Canada who provided me with an opportunity to share my understanding in working with authorities in the field. My editor, Judy Yukich deserves special gratitude because she gave me more than an edited copy, she included encouragement, the courage to continue, the foresight to express my feelings and joy in my work. I am including all the authors of the many articles, books etc., that I read while researching for this writing because although not officially cited, my learning was amplified by them. I am indebted to my family and friends for their support during my project. My deepest gratitude goes to my spouse Madeline and our children who share our lives and who have been a source of unhesitating support. Unknowingly, my family and friends in sharing their experiences in the workplace provided me deeper insight into the 21st Century. Finally, last but not least, I want to thank my publisher DBM Press for their assistance in getting this book completed and formatted into a document I believe is appealing. It was through their willingness to collaborate that this book came to fruition and I am forever grateful.

A little knowledge that acts is worth indefinitely more than much knowledge that is idle.

Kahlil Gibran[1]

Introduction

Intention and Premises

There has always been a lot of discussion and criticism about Japanese methods of management and their responsibility to harvesting human assets. The Japanese theory surprisingly stems from the American style of management of the 1940's, publicized when Thomas J. Watson, Jr.[2], the CEO of IBM wrote a series of lectures. The central premise described his belief that the single reason for corporate success was "*not technology, not strategy*, but the corporation's accountability to a sound set of beliefs." Watson believed that "respect for the individual" was most important. In the 21st century, an organization's success and failure can be measured by its ability to unleash innovation and creativity by utilizing the proficiency, collective knowledge, relationships, energies, and ability of its workforce, which will require identifying, developing and connecting people. We are possibly at a place, where introducing new human practices serves as a catapult to a company's success. All actions and decisions made in an organization are dependent on facts, but the depths of individual realization in the workplace are limited. Nevertheless, knowledge does not exist in a vacuum but is created and increases in importance from a synthesis of personal experience when combined in a group or community setting.

Companies today cannot survive, let alone prosper,

without leveraging their human assets into long-term planning and day-to-day operations. The challenge appears to inspire people to perfect their execution, skills, performance and wisdom, collaboratively working to uncover the best brain power and conduits in an organization and then sharing competence and expertise to improve effectiveness. Vast amounts of knowledge and skills lead to people being the key driver of economic impact; a term used in association with monetary worth, however, it has changed to include perceived quality, costs, personal notion, availability and performance. In essence, it is something generated earlier, that is made available to everybody in the concern who will judge it based on their preferences. As businesses strive to manage costs, align their workforces with strategic roles, increase employee productivity and efficiency to serve employees' needs, human capital has emerged as one of the pervasive elements essential for success in the 21st century. In addressing its personnel, the emphasis of the Human Resource entity has had to transform from one of not only managing its administrative side, but to also take a greater leadership role on strategic issues of managing their talent in transforming the company to address the current environment. Only with a people-focused line of attack is it possible for a company to enhance the allocation of its human assets to address new threats and opportunities. A flexible organization has to rapidly develop new skills and capabilities to meet fresh challenges from competitors all while taking advantage of its human potential by capturing, analyzing, and applying its intellectual assets faster. None of these tasks are simple as the underlying factor is the ability to identify, develop, manage, retain, and engage a capable, motivated, talented and committed workforce.

Human capital is not a fad, but a strategic weapon to help drive industry results in the current economy. A universal accepted economic theory, it has been proven that investing in its workforce and working to develop and retain valued employees will have a work society based on loyalty, honesty, trust, integrity and respect for the worker. For this reason, these companies have a forceful competitive and financial advantage. Today's corporations have a long way to go in order to make appropriate commercial gains from the intellectual assets held and generated by the employees. Simply identifying and locating their key skills and capabilities is a challenge for some organizations.

Watson believed human resources to be the essence of why corporations exist. He thought of human capital like an onion, made up of layers of sophistication of what an enterprise knows about its customers, suppliers, products, services, processes and competitors. The resources, experiences, skills, information and proficiency, developed from actual practice, are all interrelated and functioning as one for the benefit of the organization. Each layer brings its own complexity, but also a multitude of possible solutions to problems driving organizational execution and value creation.

The nature of work and the workforce have changed dramatically and are accelerating, but our institutions, policies and practices for governing and managing work still reflect the former industrial economy. Additional study shows traditional value systems within organizations are challenged, and reverence for the individual, service to the customer, obligations to the stockholders and excellence have become ways of life that can no longer be ignored. There is a stirring awareness that there is a relationship involving escalating social issues and company philosophy. The continual movement to send work offshore affects community tax bases, and the reduction of employee benefits are two examples of how employee quality of life is derailed with stress, anxiety, and frustration. Few corporations in the emerging 21st century economy are equipped to look at their workforce as a focus imperative to economic growth.

The creativity, innovation and knowledge required for an organization to maximize value creation in the 21st Century require managing a portfolio of the continuing development of its employee's intellectual assets.

A dramatic upheaval in the competitive marketplace now is prompting intense variation difficult to perceive and fully understand. If companies are to be innovative and stay ahead of the competition, leveraging and managing their human assets is vital. Given its dynamic nature, the future competitive atmosphere of technology and business will certainly continue to vary and the need for new and distinctive intellect becomes greater with each day.

Combining the difficult to define term *knowledge* with the likewise complex term *management* extends and complicates an organization's ability to improve skills and capabilities within the workforce. Organizations can incorporate the potential of its workforce; i.e. human capital existing for use in the production of added wealth, to the advantage of the whole for learning and management. Since the workplace is where people apply most of their daylight hours it is from here that an interest has been created in an organization's workforce and its precious nature. Therefore, the central issues concern human capital and the employee's ability to assimilate varying traditions, processes, input from co-workers, knowledge sharing, and technology in the organization.

A new movement for doing commerce has emerged with the intention of influencing organizational direction. A social conversion from a *values-based* approach of guidance to a *reality-based* slant began in the 1970's with Ringer[3] advocating forgetting the traditional, which had constituted a corporation's accomplishments; moral standards and values. Ringer felt values such as loyalty, trust, integrity and respect were sentimental, naïve and inappropriate for the present day competitive setting. Unfortunately, many took Ringer's

feelings to heart creating a major alteration in the current business operating environment.

Regardless of the management style however, American businesses continue to be over-run by Third World rivals forcing administration to cut costs, more often by decreasing the workforce in hopes of improving the health of the corporation. As an upshot, corporations have become so fixated with cutting costs that many have forgotten how to grow and develop new opportunities. Values such as caring, compassion and empathy are cast aside in formal business contacts. Morale is destroyed among the survivors and loyalty has become a day's pay for a day's work. Workers no longer make the extra effort, and many are even less reluctant to take risks. Work has become stressful and the worker's grief and frustrations have given in to addiction, and in some cases, violence and even suicide.

The importance of community in the workplace appears to have once again taken center stage. Such occurrences have prompted some companies to return to the paternal spirit promoted in the 1940's. John Seely Brown[4] wrote that "*When a company acknowledges the might of community, and adopts elegantly minimal processes that allow communities to emerge, it is taking a giant step toward the 21st century.*" To be a winner, corporations need a new type of direction, one willing to foster its intangible assets. There must be a realization that caring for the workforce as individuals and meeting their needs is a force multiplier. The competitive difference is found in companies where the leaders work to make their employees proactive and involved, sharing like values, questioning if what is performed is the right thing and if so is it being done right? A tactic few companies take.

I wrote *Human Capital: the Untapped Treasure,* to accomplish four purposes. First, I wanted to introduce an aspect of human capital not categorized beneath the business umbrella that it falls under, and describe the fundamentals and unique objectives that have to be addressed for the knowledge-oriented culture to advance in the information age and contribute significantly to productivity growth. Second, I wanted to demonstrate how the application of human capital is a critical determinant to productivity at both the individual and the amassed levels and describe how we can share and use what we know. Third, I wanted to illustrate how everyone has knowledge, relationships and secrets most often unsolicited and unused, resulting in lost resources to the organization. Consequently, a method for detecting the element organizations ignore must be exposed, resulting in a dollar amount lost as an enhanced corporate worth. Finally, I wanted to determine and identify what effective competencies are mandatory for leadership to be able to manage the knowledge-based output for which the worker is responsible.

My book is about *concerns* not leveraging and managing existing human capital into outcomes that could set new norms for peak execution. It emphasizes the importance for a new focus on communication and participation across enterprises since success is contingent on it. A holistic attitude with new roles and managing adjustment with a like-minded workforce collaborating intensively will be compulsory. In recent years the leveraging of the workforce has become a key topic for management intending to adapt to the changing needs of customers over their competitors. The study of human capital is a rather new topic in the business world and has become a major emphasis for research as there is a correlation involving employee development, customer-focus and profitability. Corporate mores in the present day's business surroundings should be the combination of the values and beliefs that provide direction and energy to what is done each day. This has changed however, from having the employee and community in mind, to those dedicated solely to growth, customer responsiveness, development and

increased profitability.

At one time, corporations provided housing, medical services, education, athletic fields, playgrounds, and much more, not only for the workforce and their families, but often for the communities. Conversely, today companies whose purpose it is to improve society in addition to earning a profit have developed new and exceptional characteristics, and problems with our judicial system and health care. Operating values are unique in today's corporate setting more so than in the past. Benjamin Franklin's[5] cooperation with his social network (made up of Philadelphia's city leaders) promoted and worked to establish the building of libraries, hospitals and schools. Today's social order of caring has reversed itself from a belief of *one for all and all for one,* to a belief of *each person for themselves.* My writing suggests that current corporate direction methodologies have remained management's fear of losing control in a period suggesting empowerment of the workforce resulting in ineffectiveness and the repressing of creativity.

During the initial writing of my book, fundamental traits responsible for modifications in our business traditions were determined that proved to be disturbing. A Chinese adage states "*May you live in interesting times.*" It is my belief today's businesses realize that as we progress into the 21st century, exciting times are developing as a period of immense growth. To prevail in a competitive global market where workers have become the key asset, it is essential that companies maximize their significance. The need to identify, develop and connect talent has never been more critical.

Attempts to classify knowledge can be traced to Aristotle and Socrates the Greek philosophers, who described and defined knowledge from the belief that people looked or hoped for meaning within their setting. Drucker[6] states that the skills required by today's workforce "*are similar skills to the ones Socrates referenced 2500 years ago as the keys to a life worth living.*"

Initial research for my book was the consequence of a study performed on how corporations could determine a Return on Investment (ROI) by investing in its workforce. My research over and above that of others has determined that any company investing in its workers has experienced increased operating profits and employee retention. Issues from the research amplified my awareness that companies were omitting a critical facet in their evaluation process: an understanding of what human capital they possess. The conjecture I determined was that without the acquisition and accumulation of the right information it is impractical to administer a valid assessment for ROI purposes. My research led to further study on the importance of intangible assets and the origins for new ideas often ignored by management. The real test comes with the effective locating, collecting and/or creating, sharing and applying the information placing these human assets into a repository, for later use.

Nearly twenty years ago, John Naisbitt[7] shared insights on what he believed to be the trends confronting and transforming the lives of American workers. His statement, "*the generation graduating from high school today is the first generation in American history to graduate less skilled than its parents,*" shocked and frightened many readers. As an instructor of particular undergraduate and graduate courses, I concluded that we are entering another generation where the situation may have gotten worse. Future graduates will not only have a deficiency with essential skills, but at a stage when technology is changing at an unbelievable pace, they will have difficulty in acquiring needed learning fast enough. In theory, the implication is that we are not and will not produce the engineers, scientists, and other trained personnel crucial to function in the information environment to remain dominant in a global economy. Yet, in an era of major adjustment, when workers and talent are

scarce, organizational direction appears to neglect the one resource of fundamental importance and crucial to growth and responsiveness. The prior learning, intelligence, skills, expertise and talent possessed by individual workers is never qualified, catalogued, assessed and used in their work setting. Understanding and skills are a source of sustainable long-term advantage, but leaving them untapped can prove hazardous.

After many years of studying the question of workforce stability, I believe managing talent practices can provide a starting place for altering an organization's culture. The management of human capital is not trouble-free, and this book is not meant to serve as a cookbook guaranteeing a new, improved corporate slant to life. It is a guide to help create healthier businesses.

...basically the dominant competitive weapon of the 21st Century will be the education and skills of the work force

Lester Thurow[1]

Chapter 1

The Human Capital System

Although Aristotle discussed knowledge over 2000 years ago, the emphasis is new in today's world of commerce. Knowledge-oriented terms such as *Human Capital*, *Intellectual Capital, Knowledge Base*, *Talent Management*, and *Learning Organizations* have only recently been coined. Human capital and similar terms are often used in business literature as a new model for identifying, capturing, leveraging, sharing, and applying learning to direct attention to the 21st Century workplace. Initially directed to focus on the individual, Human Capital is theoretically concerned with the recruitment, retention, and compensation involving human resources. Due to the Information Era however, its area of concern has moved onward to determining the basic skills and capabilities, identifying the existing knowledge repositories and promoting the methods for creating, leveraging and transferring human capital to meet those requirements. All in addition to retaining the key talent necessary and determining any required training and education essential to maintain and further develop workers, allowing for them to be adaptable in a changing setting.

With most knowledge in the heads of the workers and not easily transferred, it is essential that they are brought into concert through a human capital system. Studies suggest that corporate culture is a major impediment to the human capital system and it can be argued that positive attitudes toward change influence how quickly learning can be disseminated and effectively absorbed into the organization. Although the ideal practice is one where knowledge sharing is promoted, a complex and technologically sophisticated production routine requires workers to either possess or have access to the vital knowledge in order to function with greater effectiveness. A human capital system operating in a Socratic like forum, allows workers to pool their knowledge, and expertise. Learning, with and from others enables them to avoid the painful and inefficient process of individual intelligence not encountered.

Knowledge Sharing

Knowledge sharing is a process used by an individual, team or organization to inform, translate, educate, expand, leverage, transfer and apply knowledge from one setting to another. Unknown numbers of opportunities are possible when employees discover what they have in common and one aspect of an organization takes advantage of the experiences and intellect of another.

When knowledge is shared, it is somewhat analogous to Canada geese flying in a 'V' formation. As their wings are flapped; uplift is created for the geese flying behind them. Ornithologists believe this *uplift* effect extends their flight range over 70 % farther than if flying alone. The geese appear to sense that creating something persuasive is being created, synthesizing their combined efforts into even greater effort, new learning and perhaps even new possibilities. Functioning in a collaborative manner, the geese's honking serves as encouragement to greater effects and helps them to fly at the same speed. When the leader gets tired of flying, it goes to the back of the formation and another takes its place in the lead. This is an example of how leadership can be shared, something possible if there is mutual respect, honesty and trust at all times, a willingness to share problems and tasks combining and utilizing each person's abilities and sharing their knowledge. Like flying geese, workers going in the same direction, functioning as a team sharing knowledge will go through something not possible alone.

Human capital is best directed to groups and communities since most knowledge exists there. As a result, the following five distinctive facets have been identified and classified: (1) getting more from people; (2) identifying and finding critical and rare human capital; (3) building a *Knowledge Base* (4) creating new learning from accessible knowledge, and (5) leveraging all available human capital.

It was the Total Quality Management (TQM) emphasis that brought an interest in the workforce, their expertise and skills as an exponential force that could develop into a plan for taking a company into the future. Consequently, the recent movement toward a human capital based workforce gives credit to workers for knowing their jobs and recognizing their intelligence as a corporate asset and a sustainable source of competitive advantage.

The inclusion of human capital is drawn from the diverse ordinate, symbolic, and combined processes that take place in receiving new information aligned to relevant ideas existing in one's knowledge repository. By adding these methods, an individual's proficiency level is revised with each new experience, contributing further to the collective awareness of an organization. I interpret Stephen Covey's[2] statement "seek first to understand, then to be understood" as saying, the challenge of the 21st century will be to identify and create the frameworks and tools necessary to develop a deeper understanding of the behavior and attitudes that influence and undermine the way people function in today's business setting. How actions and attitudes are interpreted and reacted to, reveal whether or not they will be repeated.

Managing human capital is a problem in that as an

infinite intellectual asset it is difficult to capture and measure. Like a chameleon, taking shape and form, changing with the situation, human capital is impulsive given that it can easily get lost or mislaid. Human capital is a dimension developed by integrating internal and external expertise and the potential that provides an individual with an enhanced capacity from constructive thinking, reasoning and problem solving. Founded on interactive learning, human capital grows, expands and becomes more valuable when shared, enabling greater individual and organizational competency. As an entity that is habitually created and owned by individuals, it is seldom regarded as an asset. A flexible evolutionary resource, it is sought as an asset that can be replicated, transferred from one location to another, and widely recognized as benefiting both the individual and the organization.

Nonetheless the underlying problem begins with identifying the human capital sources and determining its merit. Although realizing where human capital exists is critical, being able to manage it is of even greater importance, and with a proper repository a manager can quickly identify how the human capital might be used effectively. At one point in time, industry could address all human capital loss with the availability of experienced and knowledgeable individuals in periods of crisis. In today's era of layoffs to satisfy cost cutting, an aging workforce, and an economy demanding new capabilities, a shortage of vital human capital has become problematic.

Human capital cannot be *measured* in the conventional sense of command and control, but if done appropriately it may be possible to significantly improve performance and productivity. Efforts to measure outcomes seemingly address only those things that are addressed in monetary terms. No standard method for placing a value on intangible assets is known, yet large monetary sums are expended to attain, sustain and retain employees believed to possess the essential means.

Depending on the situation and whether from academia, psychologists, or organizational theorists there are many definitions for human capital. Since human capital is reliant on an individual's aptitude, human capital and experiences, its significance and importance comes from an individual's ability to analyze known information into a more significant purpose. Gilbert Ryle[3], an English philosopher defined knowledge as *knowing how* and *knowing that.* His definition revealed the belief that knowledge is having the ability to perform explicit processes creating expertise and an understanding about it. Yet, Allen Newell[4] may have defined what many for centuries have attempted to do. He defined knowledge as something that can not be written, but when observed, the observer ascribes that the possessor has intelligence and will make use of information, turning it into rational behavior. To Newell, one's knowledge determined his or her behavior and that is what human capital results in – altered behavior. Neither however, really defined human capital, which for the purposes of this writing will be addressed as something more than just intelligence. It is a formation of systems, a guide for developing a standard nomenclature of skills, competencies and metrics compulsory for managing an organization's human resources today and in the future.

It is my belief human capital is a developing field that has the following synonyms; Intangible Assets, Knowledge Assets and Human Capital, all of which can be interpreted as any combination of an employee's competencies (i.e. intelligence, skills, abilities, knowledge and experience). Combined with the motivation or responsibility of applying these capabilities, an individual or organization's ability to deal with *presented* situations is greatly enhanced. Being able to deal with these situations is possible by utilizing formal (ordered and controlled) and informal (opportunistic) education, training, expertise, learning as a result of sharing (personal relationships), earlier learning, competencies and attitudes. Human capital is not something an individual is given, but something developed and learned over time and only becomes valuable enabling the organization to function if put to good use. Defining a particular term is dangerous for the reason that today's definition may not fit the needs of tomorrow and with human capital it can vary with the many applications the term is applied. The reasons for the lack of a precise acceptance of a definition are to be expected as the term may be a loose catch-all, but with human capital it is so much greater. In reality, human capital is an aggregate measure of the usefulness of personnel in an organization for performing their work and having the capacity to do other tasks to meet changing demands in the 21st century.

Since knowledge is the greatest asset an organization has, its workforce must be nurtured. Organizations with more mature talent management practices focusing on meeting the human needs of today have a more sustainable competitive advantage since it includes the ability to capture, develop, and leverage the expertise possessed by its workforce. Encouraging the leveraging and sharing expertise with new and inexperienced employees can increase their ability and magnify the worth and return from the workforce. Companies can no longer rely solely on acquisitions and mergers to expand and must work to develop and grow organically from within.

Today's enterprise atmosphere has seemingly reached a point where solving problems has resulted in diminishing returns. Repeatedly, efforts meant to reduce costs have been devastating as often the most valuable people are lost. The many corporations that have trimmed their workforce for financial reasons in hopes of improving their outlook are now trying to replenish some of the void in lost technological and innovative awareness. It has been determined time and again that corporate strategies often meant to trade off older, more knowledgeable workers, for those who are younger with less learning, expertise and skills, did not give the desired improved end results.

Another problem contributing to these losses is that often those responsible for downsizing seem to disregard certain types of human assets. The impression given suggests intangible knowledge developed from personal edification, expertise, skills, beliefs, creativity and values are of little or no significance to an organization. Levitt[5] states, "The most precious knowledge cannot be taught nor passed on," yet firms tend to ignore their precious knowledge – Human Capital. If business leaders are to believe their human resources are a competitive advantage then they will have to address their accountability differently. Instead of asking who can be gotten rid of, reduce and squeeze more out of, there should be a proactive method and continual focus on determining which of their core and non-core capabilities are obligatory to keep operating and growing. With the correct information, resourcing choices can be made based on an organization's capabilities and gaps. Only in this manner can the impact the people-related components will present them with be minimized.

Companies appear to have taken all of the possible costs targeting the workforce out of their organizations, and added reductions often bring chaos to those remaining. Theoretically, layoffs are meant to improve the efficiency of an organization by helping it curtail losses while enhancing profits. Unfortunately, this tactic (used to satisfy the demands of Wall Street and the institutional investors who are unconcerned with the soft issues) often results in fewer workers trying to perform the same amount of work. The outcome usually sparks burnout, inefficiency, conflict and low morale among employees. As this happens, a company might lose any lead it may have had over its competition. Examples of such have been experienced by corporations such as AT&T, Delta, Pratt and Whitney, General Dynamics, and United Airlines. At one time all were leaders in their industries, but all have now lost the dominance they may have had, and most are now suffering financially.

Insider information informed me that when Pratt and Whitney sought to reduce its West Palm Beach Research and Development group, it expected to lose 25 % of the workforce, but lost much more, all while it was suffering. Ironically, P & W's blunder served as a coup to other aircraft engine suppliers who hired many of those released. Repeatedly many outsourced employees are rehired; sometimes at higher wages while some businesses have paid incentive bonuses to laid-off workers to have them return, and even others such as IBM, have had retirees return as contractors at a higher salary to fill the knowledge lost. All because they later determined the wrong people had been terminated.

Business' down-sizing in hopes of improving efficiency, often end with a less autonomous workforce. Unfortunately, these new hires are apt to make safety and quality mistakes, which result in injuries, the need for rework and longer cycle-times. When the Department of Transportation investigated the rising number of Southern Pacific's railway accidents, it determined safety and quality problems were the outcome of excessive work hours demanded of the remaining workforce after downsizing.

An excellent example of workforce attenuation without strategic planning was with the year 2000 date predicament. During the preceding decade organizations worldwide had let go their legacy system's programmers because it was felt they lacked state-of-the-art technological sophistication. Yet as the end of the century approached, these same organizations scrambled to recruit individuals with COBOL programming expertise and awareness to address the Y2K issue. Remarkable, in this day of the Internet there is still a need for COBOL programmers to help integrate legacy systems with newer applications. A major portion of the world's business programs were developed and written in the COBOL language. If these programs were to stop functioning, the global economy would suffer.

I believe no new State-of-the-art software applications would have had the same meaning if the catastrophic possibilities that might have come with the midnight rollover into 2000 were examined. In an emergent situation undergoing radical transformation, could management have determined the usefulness of the familiarity and training these COBOL programmers had before they were released? Could supervision have known what human capital was present and transferred it within the organization? Could they have known what competencies lost might have offered solutions, and where could the muscle lost be found? These are questions that may never be answered.

Just how successful has downsizing been? A survey of 1,000 companies by the American Management Association found that less than half of those that down-sized had not augmented their operating profits as an outcome. Eastman Kodak, after a series of cut backs, still has problems competing with its main competitor Fuji, while Ford and GM have lost their automotive lead to Toyota.

Although studies have shown down-sizing may be futile, corporations continue to execute the process. The loss of individuals, although expensive, is perhaps a small portion of the real loss when judging how work teams are affected. The greatest loss is possibly the undocumented tacit knowledge lost with each person's departure. Surprisingly, many initial proponents of down-sizing have revised their opinions. Stephen Roach[6], Chief Economist at Morgan Stanley, like others initially believed it was the cure for any company's problems, but now considers down-sizing as a recipe for industrial disaster.

I believe companies in every concern would love to be

able to continually expand an understanding of what human capital they have as they fight an ongoing war for industry dominance. The ability to capture and utilize the human capital of their labor force would definitely represent a major leap, but organizations should realize that knowledge is not always accessible and transferable. Knowledge transfer is a measure of an organization's success with the intention of enabling people to bridge the gap between theory and application, in an era when it is essential that experience is shared. Frequently, new employees are provided minimal training due to requirement constraints, but are expected to assume greater responsibility over widened areas with little support. Knowledge is one of the few commodities that increase in meaning through use making it essential that personnel share any expertise with each other. Keeping it to oneself will reduce a company's ability to grow and excel.

Most companies judge their personnel to be an anonymous investment. Those that cut back, downsize and outsource do not sense the real significance of the individuals lost in these processes and consequently are limited in their effectiveness. Although the recent emphasis on knowledge has made it vital for companies to measure their human capital in order to advance an understanding of their resources, few fail to comprehend the vast, untapped treasure of existing knowledge, intellect, expertise and skills possessed by their workforce. Instead, they take few or incorrect measurements that frequently limit the employee's utilization and effectiveness.

Workforce reductions have become a part of shaping today's workplace. Morrow[7] writes, "America has entered the age of the contingent or temporary worker, of the consultant and subcontractor, of the just-in-time work force - fluid, flexible, disposable. This is the future. Its message is this: You are on your own. For good (sometimes) and ill (often), the labor force of the future will constantly have to sell their skills, invent new relationships with employers who must, themselves, change and adapt constantly in order to survive in a ruthless global market."

Human Capital - What is it?

High-powered transformation demands a high-octane culture, one characterized by intelligence, quality and the drive to reach the next plateau. Workers and organizations simply cannot be reliant solely on the knowledge they can create. The 21st Century playing field is dissimilar from that of the industrial era and requires highly adaptive and pro-active people. An individual's intellect, expertise, relationships, abilities and attitudes must be evaluated to determine what can be contributed by means of collective sharing and the transferring of knowledge in helping the organization. Nevertheless it does not end there. To be successful, organizations require a well-defined mission supported by objectives directed to strategic initiatives and the human capital to satisfy them. Possessing intelligence and skill does not guarantee anything, but it does provide opportunity, confidence and pride.

Although human resources may make up nearly 90% of a corporation's assets and have a major effect on a company's performance, human capital is not usually assigned a monetary value, so it seldom appears on a company's balance sheet. Nevertheless, these resources have a major effect on a company's operation. Managing human capital is a rather new science requiring new methods of measurement to determine its economic worth, but until it has monetary value it will not be saved.

Databases, documents on hard drives, e-mail correspondence and impromptu water-cooler discussions are some examples of the human capital existing outside of the realm of managed possessions. The knowledge and expertise on hand are the invisible nuggets of human capital and can be deemed as *sweet spots* in an organization. In golf the sweet spot found on a golf club is the spot at which the energy from a swinging club is effectively transferred to the ball. When the sweet spot on a club is hit the outcome is greater distance and precision, but missing the spot with the same velocity results in just the opposite. Applying the sweet spot concept to the insight of human capital, the crucial knowledge and expertise required for rapid and accurate decision-making is concentrated in certain individuals within the organization. By leveraging the knowledge possessed an organization is able to foster greater performance and productivity, both becoming dependent on the application and development of new knowledge and the leveraging and sharing by others.

Leveraging and sharing learning is a social process to facilitate a spontaneous voluntary expression of one's intellect, ability, expertise and creativity. In sharing, the sharer takes into account the incident and the context of the receiver, and will govern how the knowledge is received. Determining what is to be shared will necessitate a decision in regards with whom to interact, how it will take place and what is to be shared.

The theoretical base for the organizational intellect concepts came from the quality movement introduced in the 1980s. Consumer demands forced a greater analysis of products and services with the means by which quality was to be attained. The question coming out of this effort is, "Do the corporations have the human capital to satisfy consumers with the quality they demand?*"* Often, when a skill or competency is in demand there are insufficient quantities available to meet the challenge that will ultimately constrain the organization in need. To benefit, an organization must have the ability to understand the knowledge-level of its workforce, in addition to having the tools and methods to manage its *corporate treasure*. Human capital development begins by identifying needed skills and competencies, recruiting people to meet those requirements, and through a coordinated effort by employees networked to reach a level of consciousness make it possible to gather the human capital from those leaving. Possessing an ability to engage in a human capital development process will provide an organization with an advantage over its competitors since it can speed its creativity and ability to be innovative.

The one person best known for his work in what he refers to as the "*Knowledge Industry*" was Fritz Machlup[8], an Austrian-American economist who claimed, "The production of knowledge yields social benefits in excess of the private benefits accruing to the recipients of knowledge." His earlier writings demonstrate that he advocated the leveraging and sharing of knowledge. He emphasized that if done so; knowledge would benefit others in addition to the contributor, and as a result become human capital.

Two alternative positions come from first, Peter Drucker[9], who argued that the use of intelligence is the real capital in the systemic process of dealing with business problems. Drucker goes on to say knowledge has become today's significant resource, but unless shared, leveraged and put to use, it has little usefulness. According to Drucker, to be successful in today's environment, a company requires surroundings with *knowledgeable people*, whose knowledge is embodied, carried, applied, taught, passed, used or missed often in the workplace. The second is from Peter Senge[10] who has been credited with introducing the learning philosophy. Senge emphasizes that the problems encountered in business today are the consequences of decisions implemented to address earlier problems. His belief contributes to what Margaret Wheatley[11] describes as chaos, which she equates knowledge to a chaotic system that if allowed will approach a living organism.

Is it or is it Not?

To understand human capital, it is essential to understand the make-up of knowledge, which means something else to different people, and it is even more difficult when information and data come into play. Although used interchangeably, the debate continues as to whether they are synonymous. In understanding this difficulty it is necessary to determine their relationship, something Zeleny[12] introduced as a four-level process known as the *Data to Wisdom Pyramid,* amended to illustrate how human capital is a major part of a value-chain as shown in Figure 1.

In examining the hierarchy we see individual elements of *data* serving as the foundation. By themselves, data elements have no significance. They are simply organized, undifferentiated facts, numbers, words, sounds, or images without context and may be thought of as sand and gravel permeating throughout the organization that can be structured and captured. Rising to the next level of the pyramid, the aggregated data is placed into logical classifications, patterns, and groupings made up of both corresponding and unrelated units, so as to become useful as *information.* Given shape, the data linking and interacting in some organized form, allows it to be accessed, leveraged and transferred as one or more concepts of information. The information can be interpreted as bricks or blocks, something developed from the data, and used in making proper business judgments and helps with the further discovery of knowledge.

Although it is here where meaning begins to grow into something that can provide significance when making decisions, it is difficult to know how and when information becomes knowledge. Interpreted, analyzed and expressed as information, added valued concepts or links can direct attention to the '*who*,' '*where*,' '*when*,' '*why,*' '*what*,' and '*how*' questions.

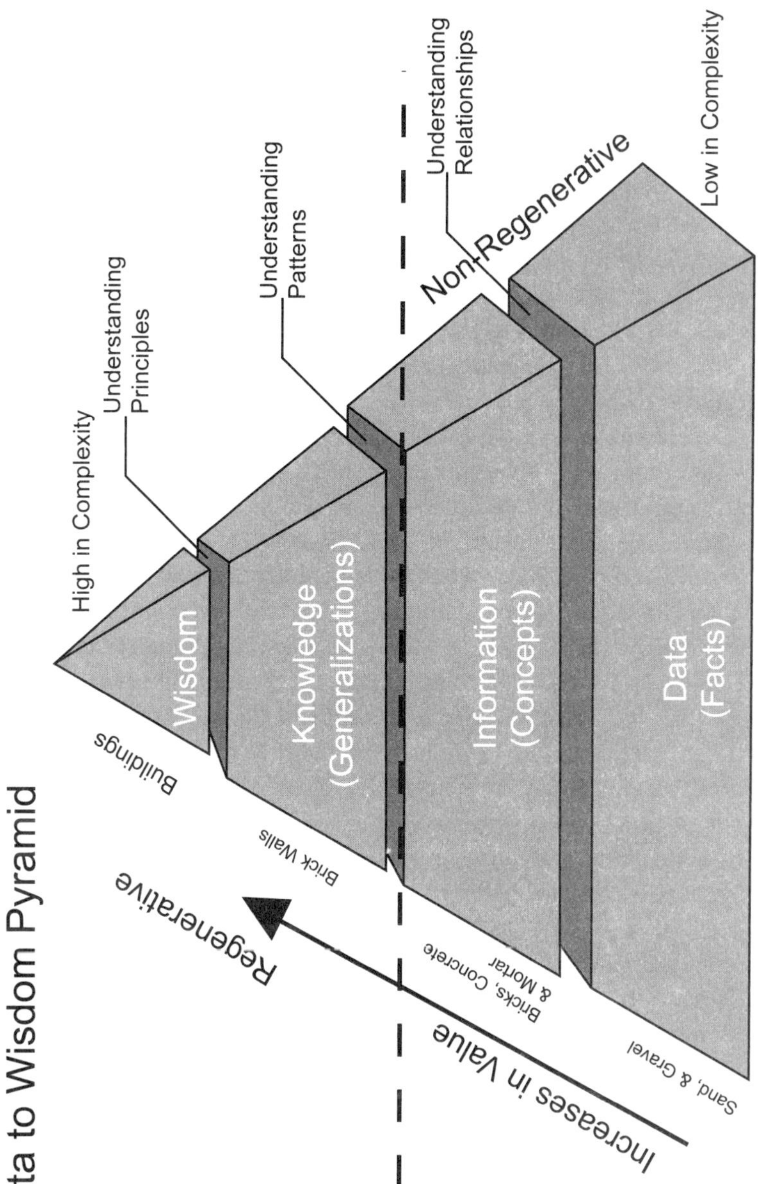
Data to Wisdom Pyramid
Regenerative
Increases in Value
Non-Regenerative
Wisdom
Knowledge (Generalizations)
Information (Concepts)
Data (Facts)
High in Complexity
Understanding Principles
Understanding Patterns
Understanding Relationships
Low in Complexity
Buildings
Brick Walls
Bricks, Concrete & Mortar
Sand, & Gravel

Figure 1

Progressing upwards to the next level of the Pyramid, information undergoes analysis and forms a basis for intelligence, productive use and action. It becomes *knowledge*, the condition of knowing as an effect of familiarity gained via experience. As knowledge, it is richer and more meaningful information that can be put into productive use, going beyond the interactions of data and information. At this level, knowledge provides relevance; an awareness or analysis of what is presented or available. To move to the next level however, will require that we tie the past to the present and then on to the future. The existing knowledge can be utilized as a foundation, which can provide valuable predictive knowledge when accessed, shared and applied in future decisions. Alone, a collection of information is not knowledge. Information has no identity or worth until it is applied, generating knowledge as an effect of the action taken.

The difference between knowledge and information can be illustrated in flying an airplane. In learning to fly one might make a purchase of some study guides, textbooks and take flying lessons. While information is what is read in books, or viewed on videos, knowledge is not the technique developed as an outcome of the lessons, but the enablers used in producing the understanding of how to *exercise* the behavior, the operational action performed in satisfying the end result - flying. Another distinguishing difference between information and knowledge is that explicit information occupies space on some media where tacit knowledge exists in the heads and associations of human resources. If information can be deemed the currency of business, knowledge is the force, with the aim of generating the currency desired as a result of the worker's interaction with the information.

During use, knowledge contracts, expands and is formed into shapes when exercised based on criteria such as the particular situation or event in place. An individual's intellect level is where his/her unconscious mind determines patterns based on their experiences, sifting through the situation presented, ignoring what is irrelevant and using what is pertinent often by means of intuition and instinct. Additionally, by answering *how* questions, patterns of understanding of predictive productive use can be brought into immediate action. Knowledge is humanistic and memory based, patterned by one's experiences and perceptions when engaged with others, all inter-connected to relationships. These relationships determine insight on how information is expected to vary and knowing what should occur when it does. Since knowledge is always in motion the patterns are brought into a result that encompasses the values, morals, integrity or principles of the organization, with the intention of reaching the ultimate level, '*Wisdom*'. The structure coming with knowledge and ultimately wisdom is *theory,* which distinguishes information from knowledge.

Without theory, knowledge has no meaning. With it a person's values and purpose unfold, as attributes, allowing change. Lacking wisdom makes it impossible to have foresight since there would be no direction for guidance, and it is with the theory of knowledge that a person's performance can be predicted and lead to greater execution. An example of operating without theory would be to blindly copy the managing practices of so-called successful *World-Class* Companies. A practice working well in one company does not mean the outcomes will be the same if implemented in another, but with a simple theory, it can have greater flexibility in making it possible to learn and develop exceptional results.

If there is awareness on *how to* create, access, analyze and use the data existing there is something of meaning present. As the *Data to Wisdom Pyramid* denotes, each higher level is the effect of some contact with the preceding lower level, and greater significance is generated with each interaction. Although data and information may not generate value by themselves, knowledge and wisdom do. Knowledge interacting with information, transforms it to an asset of greater value, enabling some action intended by a worker to benefit the organization. On examining *wisdom,* the definitive blending of intelligence, experience and judgment demonstrates the ability to discover and understand knowledge. At this point values become part of the process, helping to differentiate the compulsory actions judging between good and bad may be the element absent in business today.

Human Capital is Power

Human capital as stated, is recognized as power and a crucial driver of the knowledge process, but if shared it is even more powerful. If permitted, notable ideas come from anywhere within the organization, but it is compulsory that comprehensive and systematic processes are put in place to capture and share. Ideas themselves are not intelligence, but information that can be transformed to create additional knowledge. For information to become knowledge requires evidence that its use will effectively alter behavior. At one time it was frowned upon to display intelligence, but in today's setting of new tools, techniques and methods, the individuals with greater influence are those who transcend the limitations imposed by customs, geography and/or other reasons to share their expertise. Regardless of the idea, action must be taken to put knowledge to use. Still today's setting is perhaps at the position where too much knowledge is expected for a person to manage and even worse there is a possibility the process is too difficult to give it much depth. In actuality, there is too much information for an individual to manage by themselves.

Knowledge is not shared easily from those who have it, to those who need it. Early in our educational process we are taught to obtain and use knowledge from every possible source, but seldom are we taught how to share knowledge. Another problem might be with individuals having more knowledge than they are willing to share, for this reason it is often taken for granted. Frequently, a reluctance to withhold or not share is present when there is a personal ambition for advancement, a lack of trust, respect and honesty with those associated in the process, and a belief that knowledge hoarding might insure job security. Yet perhaps the greatest generator of waste in sharing knowledge is fear rooted in actions. By its nature human capital begins with an unknown and requires the worker to say, "I do not know or I do not understand." People are often reluctant to admit either however, as they often feel such admissions would be a reflection of incompetence and worry what others might think. It is the responsibility of managers to create a climate where workers are open and encouraged to concede they do not know, or fully understand. Collecting the competence of a few, sharing and disseminating it with others who can then use it to develop additional knowledge will generate even more authority. Unfortunately, individuals who openly share knowledge are often referred to as academic and believed to be too conventional to those who have difficulty with sharing control. It is not important from where or whom knowledge comes from, as long as it helps the organization accomplishes its goals. Researchers have estimated that as much as 80% of an organization's human capital is never applied since it is not known where it is located. Unless any human capital is identified, obtainable and used strategically there will always be limitations to what resolutions can be made. As an asset that never diminishes in value, identified human capital can represent upwards of 70% of a company's net worth. Something appealing since much human capital discussion centers on knowledge creation, but having access to acquired learning and an employee's potential for developing skills and competencies intensifies its importance. The sharing of experiences and cognition to solve problems and foster enhanced conclusions is conducive to organizational knowledge creation.

In today's business setting, influence and value are the effects of abundance and something organizations now argue and believe that if they have the obligatory information, they have an upper hand. Dr. Kuan-Tse Huang[13] stated, "*Knowledge is power . . . the power that has become the driving force in our economy. Knowledge powers our customers' ability to adapt and innovate. It powers our ability to deliver value to clients. It powers the ability of our professionals to be their best.*" Powerless individuals feel a need to hoard knowledge and control access to others and their resources. In many situations however, management appears to reward people for what they know, which encourages others to accumulate knowledge rather than share it.

Human resources possessing required intellect are the bona fide investment in the human capital society and a force that could affect an organization stimulating its development and execution. As a concern for restricting access to the Internet, McGregor[14] states human needs are organized in a series of levels, a hierarchy of importance with learning being one. His statement, *unless there are opportunities at work to satisfy the higher level needs people will be deprived, and their behavior will reflect their deprivation.* He advocated his Theory Y style of management as an invitation to innovation for the individual and ultimately the organization.

The major emphasis of Deming's[15] *Profound Knowledge* model is a commitment to training, substantiated with Senge's[16] conclusion, that learning organizations are a necessity because of today's complex global business atmosphere. The real worth of knowledge is realized when it is possible to modify the manner business functions and when workers are motivated to learn and allowed to convey any expertise to their work. They must have a desire and be committed to invest their knowledge, skills and competencies to perform superior work while making a recognizable contribution to the organization, something often not recognized. For the reason that achievement and self growth are prime motivators in today's business ambiance, individuals must be permitted to expand their human capital and thinking in order to be more creative, innovative, collaborative and cooperative in working and sharing with others.

The 21st Century business, transformed by technological, global and customer forces, must understand its true worth, which has changed to rely more on intangible rather than tangible assets, in particular human resources. Intangible assets can be turned into a springboard capable of maximizing and adding real value to the organization by extending the employee's potential. Technology no longer implies being on the leading edge: it now insinuates being on the *knowing* edge. The end result is not a passive process where workers perform tasks as historically performed; it is one where things are executed sooner and easier. Timeliness in acquiring information and the efficiency in transforming it into deliverable value-added solutions has become the differentiator for today's product and service organizations. To succeed requires that the workforce possess not only the compulsory technical aptitude, but also have the time to reflect, skills and expertise to solve problems, an understanding of how the work is performed, and to be highly flexible and adaptable.

Xerox and Buckman Laboratories are two corporations that have initiated a process that uses human capital for their benefit. Xerox implemented a process based on the activity similar to people sharing information around a water fountain. The outcome is a repository of information composed of service techniques and repair tips determined by its support staff. Any introduction and awareness of new tools enables the employee to describe what was to be performed, as described in manuals, and how the tasks were actually performed are now more accessible than ever before. In pursuing new business and providing customer service through their Buckman Knowledge Network the Laboratories operate an enterprise network of employees and things composed of electronic forums, bulletin boards, e-mail, customers and suppliers, functions others are beginning to implement.

Redefining Knowledge for the Information Age

Information Era industries require workers to expand their understanding and define their positions, relationships and priorities. Learning is highly individualized and occurs when, where and how one determines it should. Besides acquiring or improving new skills and competencies, sophistication has to lead to heightened awareness, deeper sensitivity and altered attitudes and beliefs. In order for employees to share a common understanding, a definition of knowledge, competency and human capital ought to be systemic. Competency is an individual's capacity consisting of learning, skills, proficiency and experience available for use in various situations as well as his/her network of relationships to draw from if needed. Practicing professionals have to realize that the unknown human capital inherently belonging to each individual is only shared through the organization as an effect of an employees' application.

In the Industrial Age workers could function as individual contributors whose work was public, but as a member of the Information Era social system, knowledge work has become highly private and is an open-ended series of to-and-fro collaborations, iterations and reiterations. Today's knowledge society however, leaves no room for individuals functioning by themselves. A worker requires more than human capital to do superior work. What is required is teamwork, through a social network of contacts made up of workers who are cooperative with a common purpose, values, commitment and trust. Knowledge work is not about what workers do, but how they do what they do. Consequently, competency is proven by means of relevant learning, skills, and expertise applied to the work performed.

As the term human capital implies, the human element must be taken into consideration as people are the holders of human capital and the critical aspect of business. Originating from intelligence, it is through its people that an organization's intellectual capacity is transformed into either tacit or explicit knowledge used to deliver sustainable, predictable productivity gains. All aptitude required in affecting and sustaining an advantage should reflect the accuracy of each individual worker's knowledge where differences are repeatedly not understood. Understanding the significance of human capital can be determined by measuring the contribution of each individual's unstated knowledge applied to his or her work. This will allow for determining and quantifying such things as ROI on top of the net present value of the organization. In the current setting the emphasis is seldom directed to increasing ROI, which is the effect of amplified efficiency in higher output, shorter cycle periods, new product or service introductions, higher motivation and personal job satisfaction. To arrive at the ROI desired implies that a worker's knowledge is precise, and they have the ability to replicate requisite tasks, achieving the same results and consistently producing the same significance.

Human Resources: Hindrance or Opportunity

Today, when human capital is referenced, human resources, especially those which might best be directed to maximizing the return of investment for the organization are unprepared for the challenge in addressing the key functions of attaining, developing, retaining and sustaining a productive staff. With the gradual adjustment in the workplace with workers becoming more knowledge-based over the last two decades, and altered employer - employee relations, new strategic practices are required. At one time, a relationship of *employment for life* existed, which was later altered to *employability for life,* but has now changed to what has become recognized as *employability for the present.* In essence, we have introduced the age of the contingent, temporary worker, or the just-in-time employee, who must continually add meaning to earn a spot in the workplace. With the *employment contracts* being altered in this new underlying principle of work, it is essential that HR not be obstacles to transformation. HR has a duty to become more responsible in personnel planning and effectively identifying and addressing the human dimensions essential for designing and delivering enhanced services and understanding across the company. The workforce should be nurtured by HR so they can identify and obtain a clear understanding of current talent to drive growth through measurements. With the correct information HR can review and analyze the existing work demand of the critical business processes, and determine the best technique to match the two through the integration of strategic, process and technological plans. Once completed, HR is obligated to direct attention to the appropriate training and leveraging of existing human capital to meet new challenges and opportunities. Realizing the importance of knowledge as a critical commodity, HR has a duty to become a major entity for building a responsive, adaptable, flexible and resilient labor force and not one that has to continually sell their skills, adjusting and adapting to survive. Unfortunately, HR appears to have lost touch with the human element and the worker's attitudes through the key issues affecting them.

What is compulsory is a cross-company focus that will effectively access their talent, measure their output and build the key capabilities necessary to address personal and interpersonal skills. HR must enact a development practice that will determine how an employee's efficiency and effectiveness from edification can be improved. Lacking this emphasis the company's culture will be characterized by limitations in collaboration, an increased resistance to change and less originality. For HR to thrive in its mission, several assumptions are made: (1) human capital is defined as the primary driver, and aligned to strategic initiatives; (2) the quality of training, development and the growth of talent management is monitored; (3) attitudes, and competencies are enhanced; (4) the workers are helped to develop opportunities to expand their latent (potential) intelligence through social networking and associations; (5) collaboration is facilitated across organizational boundaries; (6) employee performance is evaluated and appropriate feedback is provided; (7) development of required skills and capabilities to meet changing business conditions is driven; (8) the philosophy is one that nurtures, encourages, promotes, and rewards individuals who demonstrate innovation and exercise initiative within and beyond their primary area of expertise; and (9) policies and procedures are formulated to address the preceding assumptions.

Individual contributors need to be given planned time and the resources essential to develop the skills and competencies valuable to themselves and the organization. To meet these efforts successfully requires; (1) creating an inventory of existing competencies and maximizing their use to fill organizational gaps and/or risks losing critical knowledge; (2) gauging the employee's proficiency; (3) determining the training essential to enhance each worker's technical, administrative and interpersonal skills; (4) measuring the employee's expertise in a given competency area; (5) assessing each employee's strengths and weaknesses, to determine where each worker's competencies require further development; (6) establishing performance level standards for future recruits; (7) determining advanced functioning team assignments; (8) monitoring each individual's progress, inadequacies, creativity, potential, and effectiveness in the organization; and (9) continually assessing the significance of the labor force in the areas of performance, productivity, and promotability.

Efforts do not stop with the above described however; since management is required to continually work to develop each employee's self-confidence and respect. It is their duty to understand each employee's needs and priorities on a day-to-day basis because continual variation is constant in performance, efficiency and sensitivity. Lastly, since continual learning has become essential to maintain and further develop an employee's skills and competencies so they will be able to work effectively in the today's economy and allow them to be adaptable, they must assume a greater role in managing their careers. In doing so, workers have an obligation to continually assess themselves in determining their potential in making career choices. Therefore, each individual must take the responsibility to assess his or her strengths and weaknesses, gauge their own individual progress and growth, monitor their individual progress, creativity, and potential making career and educational decisions with the intention of affecting their future. Through assessments workers will know their standing and be able to provide insight in developing plans to realize any potential and manage their careers for professional and personal success, while increasing sensitivity to the values of their organization.

Businesses do not have the luxury to be able to replace their workforce with the introduction of each new product, service or both. The worker's intelligence should be an actionable capacity rather than a tangible asset owned by the corporation. In essence capacity refers to "the potential or suitability for holding, storing, or accommodating; competency or fitness."[17] A competency is any demonstrated characteristic or action from a learned capability or skill, and it is an organization's capacity to alter its human capital into qualifications and reusable knowledge that becomes the value asset. The upshot is something demanding the validation and utilization of the non-active and unrecognized human capital of the organization.

Companies often find themselves trapped in an unsystematic cycle in which administration is constrained from responding to their business needs with inflexible systems, a highly mobile labor force with outmoded skills and a lack of resources. Additional problems come about from a company's decision to reduce its staff, flatten, re-engineer its organizations or both, and even merge with others.

One of the fundamental skills, required by companies to sustain an advantage is an ability to establish improved levels of quality output. An example is the effort directed to *Six-Sigma*, the quality focus made popular by Motorola. Besides Motorola, corporations such as GE, Eastman Kodak, Honeywell, and Texas Instruments have recognized cost savings and quality improvements as a consequence of incorporating the six-sigma methodology. They believe their competition may eventually catch them in cost, but with the ability to respond, adapt and create as a consequence of their human capital they will have a sustainable competitive advantage in quality. Successful quality programs such as Six-Sigma are possible if people communicate well, think critically, employ (in depth) analysis and solve problems. To improve quality an emphasis on improving processes that add credibility and create new products is fundamental. Something only possible if organizations can uncover the valuable and difficult to imitate resources important in developing new methods for harnessing and making effective use of the critical human capital.

Charles Garfield[18] writes, *"skills translate as competence, pride, confidence and personal power because they [workers] are motivated to use the skills to accomplish personally meaningful results."* Most individuals have always had a desire to do what is right, because it is right for them, it makes them feel right in return and it is awareness that can provide organizational renewal, competitive dominance that has become the difference between success and failure. Consequently, it is becoming a business norm that human capital is the subtle difference required.

The Often Neglected Assets

Human capital becomes paramount and gives companies the advantage, which makes earlier competitive rules antiquated. As competition grows due to accelerating adjustments, such as in automobile manufacturing, new rules of competition are based on defining and categorizing worker's skills and abilities in order to have the highest impact. Just-in-time processing rules as an example, directed to an organization's ability to manage, adapt, renew, re-use and replace human capital from various locations are crucial to deal with the rapid change.

Traditionally, assets were determined by their accumulation. In today's atmosphere they are hastened by a company's ability to innovate and adapt in order to be more predictable, orderly, precise, flexible, and in control. To succeed requires that management be cognizant of the consequences of a company's market value when it sees:

- The loss of human capital when key folks leave;
- Costs increasing because of the number of times the company must repeatedly solve the same problem when collective expertise and deep intellect is lost;
- The rate of introduction or quality of new products and services declining;

- A decrease in productivity as a consequence of knowledge not easily obtainable;
- The lack of strategic competitive advantage in the marketplace;
- Workers confronted with constraints preventing them from sharing knowledge in the workplace; and the
- Recruitment and selection of knowledgeable, skilled workers getting difficult.

Simply knowing is not sufficient as it is imperative that administration continually work to improve the methods of identifying, developing, managing and retaining their workforce to drive new levels of usefulness. This can only be accomplished if the importance of their employee's human capital to meet the demands of an increasingly knowledge-based economy is recognized. Unfortunately, while they are struggling with this aspect, corporations are confronted with losing their institutional memory. In today's global market, business operations are now based on how well human capital is managed and deployed.

In a random survey of working graduate students pursuing MBA degrees, just one of the over 200 surveyed believed their employer was using them to their potential. The lone individual who disagreed admitted his reason for feeling different was due to his being self-employed. Although many companies reimburse employees' tuition costs, most graduates believe they will have to leave to make use of their new expertise. In a business emergent setting stressing the importance of continual growth and one in which employers need to be involved with attaining, developing and retaining their human resources, they are defeating their efforts. It is not only becoming more difficult to attract new employees, it is even more difficult to retain them.

Companies would be more profitable if they treated employees as assets to be developed rather than costs to be minimized."

Robert B. Reich, U.S. Labor Secretary[1]

Chapter 2

Human Capital – The Often Neglected Asset

Senge[2] states that the main catalyst of the knowledge movement in addressing today's problems comes from yesterday's solutions. If it were possible to capture decisions made and an understanding of why they were made, there might be a greater awareness of what should be done differently in the future. To create an environment that promotes originality and the highest level of skill usage it is vital that organizations concern themselves with past, present and future learning relying on their workforce to ensure spirited action. To survive in this era of rapid growth, geographic dispersion, fierce competition and unique cultural mind-sets, organizations require the ability to expect and react, innovate and at the same time take advantage of any opportunities presented.

A movement popularized in American industry, is directed toward decreasing the workforce assessed to be at the *lower end* of an organization's competency scale. Figure 2 illustrates the differences in the personnel categories discussed by Sveiby[3] as a theory reflecting the human capital essential for managing the company of the future.

Leaders believed to be the most skilled, are recognized as having creative personalities and are the source of supremacy for the organization's intelligence. *Professionals*, the knowledge workers who work directly with their customers in order to determine what is expected are the revenue generators. Although not as knowledge intensive as the *Leaders*, *Professionals* are valuable since they are aware of the intellect amid their areas of responsibility. These workers often prefer to function as self-regulating contributors rather than manage others. *Managers* in turn, prefer to function as part of a team, because knowing little about their customer's desires they have a dependency on others to get things done. *Clerks;* the support staff who are often unskilled workers usually lacking the expertise and skills that might place them into one of the other quadrants. This group performs essential work for the efficiency of the organization, yet is believed to be replaceable as they are usually involved with physical or mindless efforts, often referred to as backroom work. If these so-called backroom operations are determined to be of little or no usefulness to the organization, administration should make an effort to determine how to eliminate, rework or reassign these tasks to others better suited for the particular work before getting rid of those performing so-called non-essential work.

Regardless of where an employee fits in the organization, the level of adeptness in the organization and the particular job function will always be affected negatively if they should leave. An employee cutback is not unlike other management resolutions, which forces an understanding of how production will be affected if work functions are not satisfied.

Expending resources to investigate an individual's worth and then applying efforts to expand, nurture, reinforce and use these forces in an effective manner will produce unlimited benefits. Management must realize that it is not straightforward to do more with less as growing organizations are obliged to retrain and extend their human capital to do so.

Personnel Categories

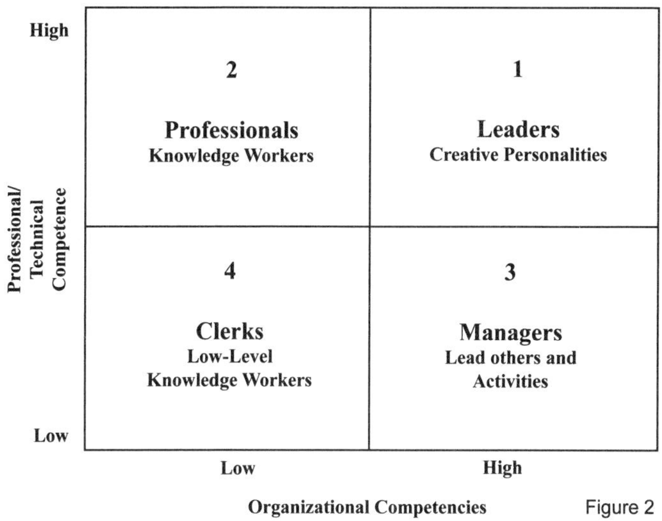

Figure 2

If organizations are to thrive and interact in an emergent competitive marketplace effective management should strategically direct human capital to drive maximum outcomes. Human capital management requires a technique of observation and analysis formulated to be used in providing an on-going alignment of people and behaviors to achieve desired results or objectives. Although not inexpensive, human capital is cheaper than having to reconstruct lost knowledge or to recover from poor decisions as a consequence of incorrect information.

New employees should be encouraged to expand and develop their capabilities, by learning from experienced workers, much like golf pros encouraging rookies to learn from more knowledgeable players. Being aware of and evaluating the pros and cons of doing particular tasks in detailed methods from the competencies of others in the workplace will result in a superior level of efficiency. Companies often seek to recruit the best personnel, pay those top wages and then tend to leave them alone. There appears to be a belief that *the best people* are self motivated to do a superior job and have the essential competencies needed to succeed. This is possibly true for an enterprise functioning in a stable setting where mobility is low and workers are provided guidance, and training and development with the aim of sustaining them in the distinct facets of the company. Conversely, in the current knowledge-based environment where findings are critical, formal strategies for creating and sharing understanding require a new corporate competency recognized as *collaboration.* In most business situations today the accelerated pace of change brings obsolescence and comprehension. Due to manpower shortages, workers are not given the opportunity to learn thoroughly enough, which poses a problem for both the employees and an organization preparing for the global economy. In hopes of alleviating this problem, some companies merge with or takeover competitors in hopes of acquiring the knowledge needed to maintain a strategic position. This may suffice as a temporary fix, but eventually they will lose any edge planned on. To bring about a striking improvement in employee execution, management must be candid in accessing and altering the methods by which work is performed. Since work has become more complex – global dealings center on people, remote workers, etc., those who need to be empowered in order to address the loss of critical knowledge. Working with HR, it is essential that organizations harness their talent and use proper measurements to demonstrate the effectiveness of any human capital programs by their commercial impact. It is essential that greater effort is directed to assure that the employees involved have the proper expertise and skills and the ability to come by new human capital for future growth.

Implementing a human capital initiative involves more

than the obvious. The initiative must include a regard for the company's traditions, its organizations and processes, all contingent on context, interrelationships, and competencies. James A. Belasco[4] states "*Great leadership is not about solving problems after the fact, but foreseeing potential problems and eliminating them before they occur.*" Having compulsory competencies will necessitate being able to manage the resources appropriately, determining when a proper adjustment in their concept of human capital is to be made, and a line of attack detailing the plans the organization has set to accomplish.

The process needed to make the human element system successful involves a balance with human resources, processes and technology, enabling organizations to effectively locate, create, share and reuse its human capital. Since socialization is a system that connects people based on skills, competencies and areas of expertise in the workplace it plays a critical role in creating human capital. Collaboration provides workers the ability to ultimately: (1) determine where information is identified and how it can be collected, captured, codified, leveraged and transferred; (2) make better decisions; (3) have faster and more accurate access to knowledge and expertise; (4) less re-learning; and (5) improved output.. This system should fashion meaning in the same manner information is presented so it can be effectively used and applied. What individuals bring to a situation is imperative, but how this information is brought is equally significant. Yet, before any information can be developed as knowledge, it is necessary to know how it is ordered, its relevance to the situation at hand and how it can be integrated for ease of access.

The knowledge initiative, although relatively new, gained importance when Ikujiro Nonaka, was named to the Haas Business School at the University of California at Berkeley as a *Distinguished Professor of Knowledge*. By establishing this position the university proved the importance of maximizing the importance of human capital and necessitating the managing of this resource in the workplace as human capital. Nonaka's appointment gives credence to Drucker's[5] belief, that we have entered into a period where human capital has become the center of the enterprise requiring a new managerial direction.

Human capital can no longer be looked upon as a person's set of skills developed over their life span, but in essence it is about strategic management organizing human dimensions that correspond to the; (1) linking of human capital in order to reduce the learning curve; (2) kind of knowledge difficult to understand, categorize and define; (3) connecting of workers in assorted geographical locations, who form complex interfaces by means of inter-connected networks; (4) connecting of relationships with diverse differences to ensure that all knowledge, skills and competencies are shared and put to productive use in supporting the functioning of current and new recruits; (5) employing of a process that will create exceptional wealth in comprehension by working smarter; (6) improving of customer satisfaction and accelerating the rate of improvement. If satisfied, these processes will transform an organization's recorded and human capital assets to the creation, sharing and managing of knowledge; in much the same method inventory is controlled.

Knowledge Types

Studies conducted by Michael Polanyi[6] examined how organizations play a crucial role in promoting knowledge, namely an employee's expertise and skills. Polanyi's studies determined that two types of knowledge; *tacit* (informal) and *explicit* (formal) are developed during an individual's lifespan. Within these two types there are two forms: (1) the ability to know *what, when, and how* to perform some task, and (2) self-knowledge.

Tacit Knowledge is personal subjective intelligence that

resides in an individual's head. Although intangible, tacit knowledge is the *knowing of something;* the wordless, pictureless competence an individual possesses. It is valuable since it is composed of ideas, assumptions, questions, guesses, stories, insight, opinions and facts. The tacit knowledge type is illusive, transitory and difficult to maintain with one's realized intellect, and constitutes an organization's memory. Made up of intrinsic knowledge; implicit knowledge is not taught, but developed through one's formal and informal education, values, business acumen and life experiences volunteered through socialization and relations. Never explicitly expressed, tacit knowledge is applied instinctively, making it difficult to articulate and share. An example of this knowledge type being applied can be perceived when observing a basketball team in action. In basketball, the allie-oop play is one where a player jumps in the air with arms extended over the basket at the precise moment the ball thrown by a teammate from a distance of twenty feet or more is directed into the basket. Another example is my grandmother cooking and baking without recipes. It was always a pinch of this and a handful of that, with no idea of how it could be broken down into exact measures of teaspoons, tablespoons or cups. Nevertheless, every pie, cake or meal prepared was just as delicious as the last.

As a resource, tacit knowledge cannot be definitely identified until it is encountered through interaction. Since sophistication is surfaced as a consequence of body and mind contact, it is difficult to transfer individual actionable knowledge gained from experience for the reason that it can never be explicitly identified. For centuries companies have theorized that it was possible to pass tacit knowledge to others if it could be observed in action. In an attempt to try and share this comprehension some attempt to do so through co-op, intern and apprentice programs.

Explicit Knowledge, the second type is formal and

systematic know-how that can be easily communicated, written or spoken. This scholarship is found in books, manuals, documents, videos and training courses used to match actions to situations. Since explicit knowledge is gained through conveyance and formal methods it is more concrete and easier to share and may best be described as *knowledge about.* Developed through factual observations and practical experience, explicit knowledge is often documented as the outcome of probing. Using the five *"W's"* (*Why, What, When, Where, Who*) and the "H" (*How),* in a situation, is one method of developing consistency. Organizations that routinely capture and rely on this awareness make exceptional business decisions. This leads to the challenge of managing human capital for the maximum benefit of the organization. Intelligence is not just the ability to recall; it is the foundation for acquiring distinctive competencies central for the development, grouping and organizing of ideas and concepts changing them into preferred attitudes. These are tools used to increase one's ability to perceive and learn, and once developed, these attributes can be integrated into a worker's everyday life contributing to his or her capability to contribute to the solving of problems. In today's business environment, it is normal to fear issues one is unsure about, but in down times efforts should be directed into developing the labor force in anticipation of things changing.

In categorizing cognition, three types of knowledge are identified: (1) *Profound Knowledge* satisfies one's social aspects, (2) *Generative Knowledge* is used to make decisions and solving problems, and (3) *Performing Knowledge*, is used in the developing of new skills, and attitudes, with the purpose of influencing ever larger circles of associates through an organization. An individual realizes only one thought or idea at a time, but once generated neither can be erased from the individual's own knowledge repository, and when extracted as unspoken knowledge they can be recalled for various situations in various ways. Connecting individual knowledge reservoirs provides knowledge available for sharing. For example, Harley Davidson's motorcycles had a reputation for oil leaks. It was a common joke that after purchasing a Harley a customer's first stop would be to a store to purchase a cookie sheet to place under the engine to catch the oil drips. After years of economic turmoil, the company implemented a continuous improvement program. One aspect of the program emphasized the importance of all staff participating and sharing their wisdom. As a result, a maintenance worker stated she had the answer for correcting the drip problem. She had known the solution to the problem for some time, but no one had ever asked her for input. Her input helped the company in resolving the problem at a small cost per motorcycle. In the same manner, the indispensable knowledge to solve many of today's problems may only require locating, sharing and leveraging.

Improving operational efficiency and effectiveness requires imagination, which if used properly is a powerful method for attaining and creating knowledge from outside of one's functional area. Imagination takes into account the gamut of all possibilities, contacts, bygone and future, real or possible. Regardless of the human capital possessed, it is essential that it is used to generate greater amounts. Nonaka[7] believes knowledge creation is the outcome of the four possible interactions as indicated in his Knowledge Creation model identified in Figure 3. The first interaction of *Tacit-to-Tacit* knowledge is the *Socialization* phase. This phase synergizes the combining of unexplainable knowledge from numerous combinations. The feeling of knowing what someone wants or needs and how to satisfy them without having to ask is an example. *Tacit to Explicit,* the second phase is *Externalization*. Here, tacit knowledge is shared and combined with explicit knowledge that provides improved administrative abilities when expanded. *Explicit to Explicit,* the next interaction is known as the *Combination* phase, where the bringing together of knowledge is executed through multiple, diverse sources and social processes, which increases the probability that human capital will be transferred to others. Communications and collaboration spanning the organization during meetings and telephone conversations is the end result of this phase and one of the most effective methods of sharing. The last interaction, *Explicit to Tacit,* is the *Internalization* phase in which explicit knowledge is articulated throughout the organization. The outcome of this interaction is internalized and expanded implied knowledge that may originate outside of the organizational boundaries by others, and made their own by other workers.

Knowledge Creation Model

	Tacit Knowledge	Explicit Knowledge
Tacit Knowledge	Socialization	Externalization
Explicit Knowledge	Internalization	Combination

Figure 3

Workplace savvy is by and large the product created from the relationships of tacit, explicit and a third type recognized as *organizational knowledge.* This knowledge is developed as an effect of the various associations gained from the many sources of information in the organization, but mainly through communications. Aligned to an organization's culture, beliefs, values, attitudes, operating philosophy and accountability, organizational awareness defines its meaning and shared values.

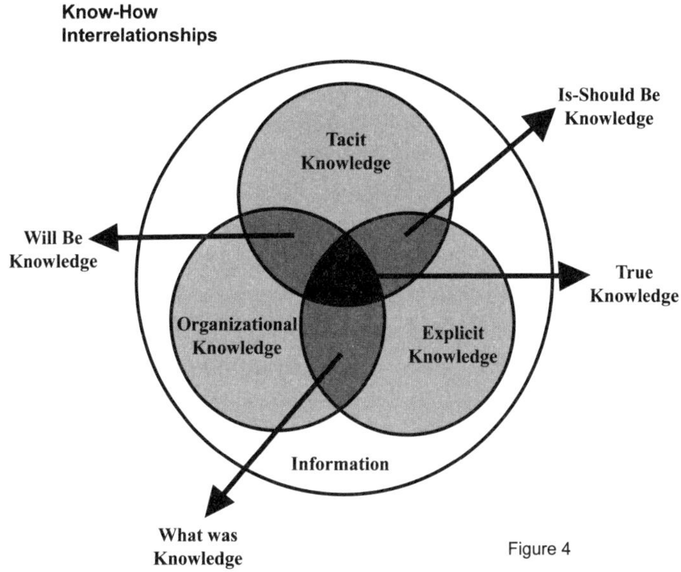

Figure 4

The force of understanding comes from a person's ability to share his or her knowledge and then converting any tacit knowledge to explicit and organizational knowledge. Converting an individual's know-how can be seen in the Venn diagram depicted in Figure 4, which addresses four possible interrelationships:

The first knowledge interrelationship *Is - Should Be*, is the outcome of tacit and explicit knowledge interacting with one another, which ultimately creates new, explicit and expressive knowledge. In the *What Was* interrelationship, explicit and organizational knowledge interact creating *declarative* knowledge when combined, something attained out of formal training and education. It is this learning that allows workers to develop an awareness that something must be done, but they are unable to do so because of the lack of skills and technological competencies, which leads to the third interrelationship, the *Will Be*. This interrelationship is what identifies the learning developed as a result of tacit and organizational knowledge interacting. The outcome of this action is the perception, intuitions, attitudes and values applied against organizational processes, procedures and policies identifying requirements. At this point an individual can transform and deliver his/her awareness when and where it is needed. The fourth interrelationship, *True Knowledge or Wisdom,* is the outcome developed from all types interacting. The outcome is in response to the knowledge created when sharing a concept with others who can sense what is being articulated. With true intelligence or wisdom the meaning or analysis of intangibles is understood. Intangibles are the tacit knowledge blended with one's individual aptitude and attitudes. It includes the knowledge of others that although not well articulated determines their competency, enabling them to perform work tasks successfully.

Organizational Knowledge Characteristics

Organizational human capital is comprised of four types of characteristics. The first can be titled Band-Aid knowledge, which is used on impulse or without solid validation in hopes of resolving problems or decisions, but is often ineffective or ignored. The second characteristic, *craftsman or artisan* knowledge is personal learning, commonly associated with specialized know-how and expertise. The end result of this characteristic is usually what is expected. *Newly created* knowledge, the third characteristic, is based on a process and usually validated by the belief it is functional. The fourth and last characteristic, *Prior or Acquired* knowledge, is developed, accumulated and adapted due to exposure and practical experiences faced and learned by individuals. Much of the aptitude individuals have can be referred to as acquired understanding. The significance of this comprehension will depend on how much can be recalled, used effectively and directed to creating additional awareness.

People are motivated by the desire to make a difference in the world around them. Although awareness out of experience provides a method for creating a meaningful atmosphere, workers are seldom involved with problem-solving and decision-making in their areas of responsibility. This is surprising, as workers know their jobs better than anyone else. Still they are obliged to learn the knowledge already known when performing a task for the first time, and this widespread occurrence raises several questions. How much will it cost for an organization to re-learn something already known, and if the organization is directing all of its resources to re-learning, what might it realize if the unused human capital was directed to developing new products or service?

Invisible Assets

The American economy in the 90s suggested that management was able to generate greater efficiency from its human resources than ever before, much of it as the effect of the development and application of new learning. As successful as management was, organizations could have had greater success if acquired knowledge, the one asset they showed little interest in, had been better managed and leveraged.

Not all knowledge can be captured, but if captured, it may not be transferable. To be of value the organization must know who has it and its reliability. Identifying who has what knowledge will allow the organization to effectively use the competencies and ability of others while producing additional capabilities, enhancing productivity, advancing learning and ultimately generating innovation. In today's work setting, management should always be in search of the workers who have the compulsory competence to take the organization to the next level. Organizational leaders have to determine how to identify and articulate opportunities, and utilizing understood knowledge readily accessible would be one such innovative process. Focusing on and managing the inconspicuous human capital definitely helps with the creating of additional opportunities for the reason that it is this human capital that is developed and expanded with experience. The complexity is perhaps in controlling the precise awareness.

Cognition includes a combination of an individual's pre-existing skills, competencies and attitudes. It is developed based on experiences and understanding retained and transferred from former dealings before an operation can be performed, and the newly created realization due to the operation. This definition implies a strategic resource upon which an organization can either act or collect additional might to expand its strategic ability. Not looking at prior learning occurrences can be dangerous. Knowledge begins with the individual based on communication and interventions with others. From these interactions new mental models can be developed from organized learning in preparation for the next educational process. An individual's memory is altered repeatedly with new learning and this continual updating enables workers to retool themselves as required.

Realizing the importance of eliciting newly developed knowledge, which is often the consequence of implementing quality initiatives requires organizations to preserve and harness any human capital which may have been generated by the multiple contacts involving their customers, suppliers and peers. The rate by which organizations elicit knowledge will determine any competitive dominance, but it is crucial they continue developing with the intention of being a valued contender. A head start can come through the use of acquired learning; the priceless resource often ignored, unrecognized and lost due to the lack of usage, but is never used over new learning.

Experience has always been the major element for augmenting problem-solving. For example, in the mid 1980s when some Tylenol containers were tampered with, Johnson & Johnson made a decision to openly publicize the situation and pulled all Tylenol products off the store shelves across the country. Its customers accepted the situation, and as an upshot, Tylenol has remained a viable product while maintaining its customer base. J&J's process of notifying customers has become a landmark example, which has since been used by companies in similar situations proving that harnessing and using cognition may provide an advantage over the competition.

By not looking at the existing information companies will inevitably create animosity with customers and ultimately affect their bottom-line. Airlines have ignored this line of attack, and have received recurring criticism about the lack of information shared regarding delayed flights and even accidents. These companies are seemingly fixated on their own needs and are often reluctant to work on improving a process which might help in generating public trust.

General Electric and Wal-Mart are two major U.S. corporations that have leveraged earlier learning to create or improve processes so as to benefit the organization and the individuals involved. GE's *Workout* process involves teams of workers presenting ideas for improvement to improve processes or eliminate non-value added work in the workplace to managers for evaluation. Workout is similar to the Quality Circles used by the Japanese for improving processes except the size of the group involved may be larger in number. In either process, once an improvement has been implemented, the groups disperse and members may or may not get involved with other improvement processes. Wal-Mart similarly, has developed a process known as the Quick Market intelligence process, which has revolutionized the retailing industry.

This particular method helps manage human capital, which is more difficult to manage than physical assets as processes do not perform the work, people do, making the method used mostly informal and spontaneous.

Expanding Human Capital Value

Human capital is truly the hidden value of an organization. When mature employees in their fifties leave an organization, their twenty plus years of competency does not magically transfer to their younger, less independent replacements. Their knowledge is an outcome of experience, and overlooking this aspect implies a necessity that it be recreated, which requires time, resources and possibly other actions.

There are problems in the workplace however, with the dynamic, changing markets, continual technological and generational differences. Unless there is more understanding of these differences there will be less flexibility, continued frustration, lack of trust, and reduced production. Many studies reveal that mature experienced employees tend to demonstrate higher creativity, improved performance, greater productivity, reliability and more wisdom than those who are younger, and less self-supporting. Furthermore, older employees are usually more reliable, responsible and committed. Therefore, since knowledge is learned as a result of experience, aging might be thought of as a state of growing, giving the more mature employees the ability to understand their limitations and differences difficult to detect. In examining the generational differences we must understand that the older more mature employee is protective of his knowledge and expects resolutions to come down from management. The younger employee in turn is more concerned that any knowledge will help in advancement and is more collaborative with problem-solving choices. An example, illustrating the relationship linking acquired and new learning involves a major utility company in Florida.

The company was experiencing a prohibitive number of electrical outages due to transformer blow-outs. The company formed teams to determine the cause of the blowouts and one team included several rather new, younger employees and one older long-service employee. During initial meetings however, whenever the question of whether anyone had ideas as to the cause of the blow-outs, the long-service employee would respond that frogs were the reason. His comments would cause his teammates to frown, make unkind remarks, often referring to his age. After being ignored on several occasions the man came to the next meeting carrying a six-foot wooden plank with a dead frog secured to one end and a transformer terminal light to the other. To satisfy the other team member's interests the man explained that whenever it was humid (especially before and after a rain storm), insects would bunch up around the terminal light. In search of food, frogs would lash out at these insects with their tongues while seated on an ungrounded area up to six feet away. Ungrounded while extending their tongues in an attempt to catch an insect, the frogs would frequently cause a transformer to blow-out. As a result, engineers developed a shield to place around the terminal lights and the number of blowouts was significantly diminished. Other utilities have since leveraged and incorporated this awareness. Learning from others helps in creating new knowledge and through value creation processes expand the organizational human capital base. It should be noted that the man was treated with greater respect by his teammates after his contribution.

Once developed, human capital can be reused. The odds are high that the expertise, knowledge, skills and competencies possessed by workers performing any work have already been paid for and are available resources for reuse. By utilizing readily accessible and proven knowledge workers can ideally work with superior speed and efficiency. The real problem comes when capturing acquired learning or *organizational memory* developed from practice. Organizations able to harness this learning have a sustainable advantage over other organizations with an ability to make decisions in a rapidly changing workplace.

In his February 1997 letter to GE shareholders Jack Welch emphasized the importance of learning and expanding the company's horizons to better support it. His statement to "continuously learn from any source and rapidly convert this learning into action," supports a similar belief expressed by W. Edwards Deming[8] in his *Theory of Profound Knowledge*, which advocates the importance of continual learning in order to prepare for adjustment. A second statement by Welch "*Reward the finding and sharing of ideas - even more than their origination*," indicated the importance and necessity of both lateral and vertical collaboration and sharing across organizations as success factors for innovation. Fostering a collaborative environment has become critical for organizations trying to learn, make decisions, solve problems, working on common projects, developing new products and services and growing through innovation, but many are still unprepared on how to manage the process.

Elton Mayo[9] discussed the importance of sustained support. For collaboration to be successful, it is imperative there is a process for the knowledge acquisition, identification, creation, assimilation, dissemination as well as its leveraging, sharing and application to achieve competitive advantage. In addition, to providing desired awareness, this action will result in the creation of a new comprehension application when called upon and reuse when required. Taking advantage of knowledge reuse will help in easing costs and in developing alternatives. If this mechanism can be incorporated into the organizational culture, immediate benefits will be recognized.

An example where earlier learning produced remarkable outcomes involved the near disastrous Apollo 13 moon mission in 1970. Mission control assembled a team of engineers to help resolve a problem with the space shuttle's carbon monoxide scrubber. The team tapped into their treasure of cognition and developed a creative solution which brought the mission astronauts back to earth. For organizations to create real consequence for the 21st century enterprise will require a process where peer production is the outcome of harnessing the hidden local expertise embodied throughout the workplace and bringing it to the surface is critical. Like muscles in the human body, knowledge will develop and expand if exercised. Understanding and combining another person's depth of expertise with one's own will help strengthen the abilities of those less knowledgeable and experienced.

Answers to any company's problems exist somewhere in the workplace with someone who has the right combination of knowledge and experience. It is the identification and use of an organization's human capital that will determine how successful an organization can be. The more skilled and autonomous a workforce is will; (1) determine the size and merit of its knowledge repository accessible; (2) allow for the reviewing of added earlier experiences, thereby enriching all new learning when performing tasks; (3) permit the engaging in new deliberate practices; and (4) provide more informative feedback to improve their actions.

Lessons learned by the method of problem solving can provide organizations with energy and influence since they serve as stepping-stones to new learning. When new instruction is combined with competencies in a precise set of circumstances, it can revitalize a person's mental frame of reference so all new knowledge can be used strategically. From here, modification in knowledge, skills, competencies and attitudes begins to affect ever-widening circles of individuals, leading to corresponding alteration in individual behavior. Any variation exhibited by those directly involved in the activity will influence alterations in any operation leading to concrete changes in the manner things are done. The changes are noticed by others, and if accepted, will support the new methods of execution. Indeed, this level of support increases to where the differences become institutionalized, and since knowledge grows exponentially it can be a major asset in the development and support of work functions.

Some persons make the grade where others fail because they are able to maximize any gained learning. For example, a friend went to have his eyeglass lenses tinted. The optician took one of the lenses from the eyeglass frame, dropped it on the counter and informed my friend the lenses could not be tinted. When my friend asked for additional assurance, the optician asked a fellow employee to verify her findings. The second optician repeated the process, and stated since the lenses were made of polymer plastic it was not possible to tint them. Confused, my friend asked how a decision could be determined by just dropping the lenses on the counter. The opticians explained that their conclusions were based on the sound generated from the lens hitting the countertop. The sound was similar to that of a plastic poker chip dropped on a hard surface, whereas the glass lens when dropped on a similar surface would give a lower pitch. The opticians could recognize the difference in the sounds generated from repeated dropping of lenses on the counter tops. Cognition assimilated with that of the present can prove to be valuable in its usage so it can be an inspiration for creativity and may come close to becoming wisdom. It is this elusive earlier knowledge that makes the difference in today's competitive atmosphere.

New Criteria Goal

The criterion essential for the 21st century workplace is the ability to locate knowledge considered essential. Known as *knowledge navigation*, this process includes identifying, eliciting, codifying and leveraging essential know-how to solve problems and make decisions. In doing so, a worker should have direct access to the human capital, which will make it possible to break down and solve problems in ways initially not likely and allow solutions to be reused in other applications. This will require an organization to inventory its human capital and organize it so it can be accessed in the most efficient manner.

Technology has helped increase information, but it has done little to assist the user. Storage of information has amounted to a glut stored for fear it might possibly be obligatory sometime in the future. Consequently, many organizations discover themselves trapped. The pressure from changes in technology and business makes the need for new competencies greater. Workers are constrained from responding to organizational initiatives by their inflexibility; outmoded skills and the lack of time contributing to their feeling entangled. This constraint is just one of the reasons many workers feel trapped and display attitude and behavior problems in the workplace, often leading to absenteeism, illness and turnover. Many of today's workers dislike their jobs and four out of five change careers, some several times during their work life. Repeatedly, many switch jobs for the reason that they believe any contribution to the organization has no real purpose. They strive for perfection, but if unhappy it is displayed in their actions and poor quality in output. The measure of an individual's development should be a noticeable or measurable behavior modification on the job, such as improved customer-focus and interest in their work.

Old business rules in a knowledge-based setting are no longer valid. Work must be re-oriented around human capital, and companies being innovative and having the ability to authenticate their products and services sooner than their competitors will have greater success. This will also require new business models and a labor force aware of how things are executed, and the technology to help nurture and make effective use of the human capital while focusing its resources properly. As a culture, organizations do not suffer from the lack of knowledge, talent or motivation; it is from the lack of not using this capability. To have greater efficiency it is imperative that management shift their requirements from a *Push* system in an attempt to forecast and spread their awareness to a Pull system, involving the sharing and use of best practices learned. In a desirable system, workers are able to assess and consume hidden human capital, which may be even more advantageous. Workers with the greatest number of options to any situation are most likely to achieve their outcome.

Organizational culture and human capital are synergies, and have to be affected in supporting new attitudes and behaviors. An organization's customs is what stands in its system of change. If there is a desire to join the *knowledge torpedo-train*, a new technique where everybody works in a collaborative manner is crucial to encourage the alteration. A new culture where employees are committed and satisfied is essential in bringing about new creativity directed to the harvesting of new knowledge. This will help create a social network supported by technology directed to a brighter future.

Human Capital and Organizational Strategy

Strategy is dynamic and adaptable. Historically regarded as a military concept, it has been characterized as the use or the threat of combat for the purposes of war. Today, strategy might be defined as the usage, or the threat of a lack of advantage for the excelling of others in something and everything for sustainable competition. The focus of human capital management strategy should be directed to the high-level, overall orientation and drivers of the organization, with the aim of ultimately transforming the worker into a competitive resource. Additionally, this concentration should be about channeling an organization's resources, integrating the positives and multiplying them to attaining superior execution, all directed to its core mission and the creating of value for customers.

As a new strategy, *human capital* should be a never-ending journey, not a defined destination, bringing to light the dormant knowledge of an organization. An infrastructure will be essential to convert this strength into a value-added resource, but it does not end there. Once an organization creates a mindset promoting sharing and collaboration, it will require new ways to implement the best human capital processes possible.

Although a theory, human capital is gaining in popularity and remains an under-developed system in which all assets, tangible and intangible need to be included. Human capital must be developed as a new, strategic system because an organization's human capital is found in diverse sources defining the business. I believe events, which consume and produce knowledge activities are found in companies able to conceptualize new ways for utilizing human capital such as:

1. Incorporating the understanding and effective measuring of knowledge.
2. Capturing and bringing together knowledge, (i.e. acquired learning)
3. Generating and creating new knowledge
4. Assimilating the knowledge captured, codifying its content and storing it in an accessible structure
5. Disseminating the knowledge through its leveraging and sharing for value-added benefits
6. Determining a strategic usefulness for the knowledge

7. Knowing and understanding what the competition is doing by means of its human capital

It is natural for businesses to strive for an advantage over any competitors, and with a strategic management process this is possible. The strategic use and effective measuring of human capital is essential to a company's ability to effectively compete and survive. This will require learning incorporated into the organization to increase its value, something difficult given that harvesting knowledge is conditional on context, and to do so effectively will require acquiring savvy from assorted areas at a measurable rate of speed and ease of use.

The emphasis to encompass learning into the organization is possibly shifting to one of combative strategy with the retention of a skilled workforce becoming critical to the workplace. An organization's ability to attain and sustain the best in a diminishing market is coming to the forefront of management attention because of the shortage of skilled workers in a growing and changing market. Some industries in health care, education, energy and utilities, hospitality and information technology are growing so fast there is a need for technologically skilled workers.

If management is to transform their businesses into growth oriented organizations they have to recognize the need for creating knowledge. In order to do so, the core competencies, the value-creating skills and capabilities by which an organization can access and share its levels of knowledge must be known. Many companies are beginning to realize that the expertise attained to solve problems may have relevance and commercial significance. According to employment experts many appear to be relying more on the competencies such as problem solving, quality control, process improvement, research, and customer service possessed by mature experienced employees. In today's competitive setting, collective knowledge is essential to the success of companies focusing on producing quality work while working to improve efficiency and reduce costs. This technique means accomplishing higher quality work, using fewer resources, and doing so smarter with greater speed. An example is seen with the utilities working to retain experienced workers who have been through crisis situations and know and understand how to deal with catastrophic events.

Management has been modest in efforts to understand the needs of workers in developing knowledge. Consequently, little has been done to determine the human capital possessed by individuals and the organizations to which they belong. Business leaders want to measure improvements, but appear to look at the workforce primarily as costs to be lowered, rather than resources in which to invest. They neglect to measure the effect and worth of any development and outlay for employees, and usually cut training and development budgets first when business operations come under cost pressure.

The business scheme crucial for existence intensifies the emphasis on developing the knowledge of human resources. Since training and development have become issues of major significance in raising the skill and competency levels, which ultimately leads to higher productivity, adding merit to an organization's status requires that it be part of a company's strategic plans. Many are still in an introductory phase trying to evaluate the effect and meaning of training and development on their business. The compulsory training and development cannot be carried out using long-established methods. Training meant to solve a problem, overcome a deficiency or prepare employees for an accurate requirement must now also prepare them for the future by supporting and developing their ability to execute in the present. The development process requires new methods, tools and processes to speed up learning, generate elevated skills and competency levels, optimize execution, enhance comprehension and stimulate behavior and attitude. It is essential that greater attention be paid to invisible capital, because of the methods required for valuing human capital developed. The tools determined should help managers identify; the skills/competencies on hand in their community; copious ways on how to use them; which of them requires developing and lastly, how to measure ROI.

Once an individual's knowledge level is determined, combined with an understanding of any requirement in their development, the organization can establish a monetary value. Assessments of financial costs versus benefits will determine the success of training if the effects produce a measurable ROI business affect. One possible method for determining ROI can be approximated using the following equation, which basically states all ROI is attributed to the outcome of intended learning as the outcome of training, less the cost of such.

ROI = (Value of Benefits - Cost of Training)/ Cost of Training

Besides collecting and disseminating knowledge, management ought to create systems that stimulate a networking mechanism for communicating with other members of the organization in order to share ideas and edification. In actuality, organizations can be regarded as a mechanism, which allows the workers the capability of acting on their human capital by exchanging ideas and creating problem-solving solutions. Since employees are a major source of knowledge and new ideas, and human capital is developed as the consequence of people-to-people contact through a social capital relationship with others, a principal influence by which functioning and learning is made possible.

Today's workplace requires that workers have; (1) a fundamental understanding of reading, writing, and arithmetic; (2) the ability to work well with others; and (3) the potential to listen, negotiate and communicate. These skills, once believed to be a necessity for decision makers, managers and supervisors are now essential at all work levels, which will require new relationship building skills often not found in today's business state of affairs.

The United States Department of Labor estimated over 80% of the work performed in the United States would require the use of cerebral skills by the mid 2000s, and more than 50 Million of these workers would be knowledge workers[10]. It is possible these projections have already been exceeded, but whether or not; to achieve this operation level will rely on the ability to consolidate intellectual assets and align them with defined core competencies in support of the corporate plan. The effect is meant to produce a unique labor force, smaller in size, but one that is more energetic, capable and knowledgeable.

Human capital is definitely concerned with numbers of workers, but it begins with the individual. The success of a human capital strategy requires that workers know and understand the organization's strategic objectives and those with whom they work. In today's background, one where every person is expected to do more with less, many businesses lack the planning required to address the increasing levels of competition.

To maintain an elevated level of organizational effectiveness, workers must be trained with the skills, competencies and learning vital to remain competitive. This is possible if organizations are linked to their workforce through nurturing and optimization, while striving to improve their development and operation. Basically, what we are referring to is workforce performance management. This is a process where continual learning, the application of measurements, assessments and tracking the intangible qualities helps an organization increase its understanding and determining the usefulness of its human capital.

In today's information age, managing collective human capital as an asset has become a necessity. Only human capital or the totality of knowledge, technological capabilities, individual expertise, attitudes, and performance of the personnel, can bring an organization to a world-class level of execution. Utilizing this cumulative competency correctly in a flexible work setting will encourage effectiveness leading to enhanced organizational influence made possible by matching the right people with the right skills to the right roles with the right information. Coupling the human capital of each member of the workforce with that of the organizations will increase it exponentially making knowing who invaluable. In order to manage and measure human capital, an awareness of an employee's proficiency level against predetermined levels of ability to perform a task is vital. This has evolved into an emphasis known has talent management.

The upheaval in the social, technological and cultural aspects of today's business state requires that an upside-down or out-of-the-box thought process be put into action. This will require managers to redesign and develop new processes to encompass all areas of today's involvement, to chance upon a path to continued development and progress. By re-engineering their collective knowledge resources, management may be able to foster organizational needs and requirements, but it is the innovation process used for transforming ideas that lacks the understanding to be managed.

I believe the real difference between success and failure in a corporation can very often be traced to the question of how well the organization brings out the great energies and talents of its people.

Thomas Watson Sr. [1]

Chapter 3

Improvement Will Require Transformation

Although, customer-focus is the supposed direction, companies seemingly do little to direct efforts to remain competitive, with many directing their technological resources solely to the financial aspect of the business. The reason for this lack of extension to other areas is management not understanding how workers today are to function in the areas of communications, operations, collaboration, leveraging and the sharing of know-how. This is the result due to the lack of training on knowledge flow and its creation with its biggest problem possibly being the time needed to determine the human capital obtainable and how it can be shared with others. Information has always been passed to others throughout history, whether by messenger, telegraph, telephone, a delivery service, communications via computer and satellite. The difference has always been the method used to transfer the information from one location to another. One such example was the Pony Express. Getting mail coast to coast in 23 days by horseback was without doubt an improvement from sending the mail via stage coach requiring months. Yet changes such as these were not without problems as man-to-machine relationships were introduced. Workers became uncomfortable when they believed machines were usurping their importance. Machines were initially regarded as the prime capital asset, to which the worker was found to cater, and the worker although in control was interchangeable. With the Pony Express, the horse was the machine, and of greater importance than the rider. Workers were pictured as automated creatures as part of the machine instead of the machine being an extension of them, and as such work was found to be unappealing and unsatisfying.

Changing emphasis, from the industrial to the Information Era, occurred around 1980, when technology and the personal computers made the transition for acceptance and acknowledgment sooner. The Information Era brought with it a shift in importance, as the human element became the prime asset, as seen through the new version of the Pony Express; with companies such as FEDEX, UPS, DHL and Airborne Express. A route person for any of these can be responsible for millions of dollars of business, and this requires a special type of person; one who is open, flexible, willing to share, collaborate, and has interpersonal and communication skills with an understanding of Business Acumen.

Preceding the Industrial Age, knowledge was shared by oral means, such as mentoring, storytelling and apprentice programs initially focused to behavioral and skill development. Today, these methods are used as a means of transferring knowledge for retention from a more experienced, aware worker to one who may lack in knowledge, skills and experience. These methods often involved a special one-on-one relationship where an expert's familiarity was passed by means of practice, observation, problem solving and experimentation. The shift to human capital revised the importance from the tangible (machine) to the intangible (human capital) and by means of their attainment, capture and application that gave the worker relevance. Separating the worker from the machine resulted in an extension of the worker's capabilities focusing on output and introduced concerns on job satisfaction, innovation and creativity.

Technology can help with the growth and nourishing of knowledge, but it is imperative that it is integrated into the business plan as a system for the elicitation, capture, understanding, categorization, assimilation, leveraging, sharing and creating of new knowledge. It is not the final answer however. It works well when it works, but when it does not perform as desired it can be catastrophic. The dynamic and volatile nature of work technology has varied since the advent of the global marketplace. Today's worker is required to address the challenges with greater complexity as a consequence of change, and stronger global workforce integration is only possible if technology is used as a tool. Nevertheless, technology is not enough; to be responsive in satisfying today's market requirements, an organization must integrate technology, processes, knowledge and expertise across its functional units to make a difference.

Human Capital Application

It is believed only about 3 - 20% of the human capital in an organization is used. By expanding the ability of those who structure the organization, each individual's influence through the organization will also expand. Alone knowledge is inadequate in the workplace, but the action one can take based on its availability is critical. It is difficult to imagine what an organization might be capable of doing if it employed just 5% more of its existing human capital.

People have the ability to be creative, but will lose proficiency if their expertise is not applied. This is made possible when the atmosphere is congenial and supportive, and one where workers have trust, faith and are cared about. Surroundings such as this will encourage workers to be open, willing to share and leverage human capital. By helping workers develop exclusive combinations of qualities and capabilities an organization can benefit from a return owing to enhanced operation and higher productivity. As such, human capital enables an organization to use its other resources to adapt and create. This will require knowing where to look and how to analyze information for improved decision-making.

Harvesting Human Capital

Human capital may be looked upon as a system consisting of four distinct processes as illustrated in the *Harvesting System of Human Capital,* in Figure 5. The system establishes human capital as a process to make knowledge-aligned activities such as the acquisition, creation, assimilation, and their dissimilation possible. The first phase of the cyclical system of harvesting human capital begins with *Acquisition*, a process where knowledge, which includes e-mails, digital files and the like, and skills are identified, collected, codified and stored from a variety of internal and external sources in a format or structure so this information will be available to others when they need them. This may entail integrating the information into manuals, posting it onto the internet or a web site, and/or knowledge warehouse. Seeing as knowledge is difficult to articulate, develop and transfer, it is important that an organization identify, understand and determine the value of its human capital before its importance will increase.

Knowing *where* untapped knowledge exists in the organization relies on socialization to determine who may have the unspoken knowledge, and what value can the human capital generate for its customers is all a part of the *Acquisition* phase. A measurement method will be required to proactively improve the process.

Harvesting System of Human Capital

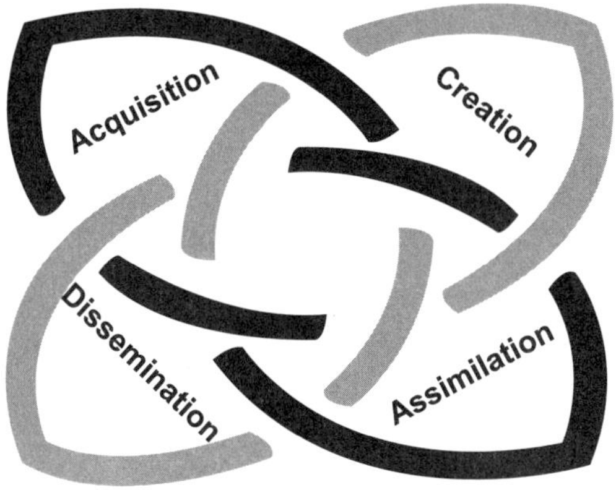

Figure 5

Technology's rapid development is providing unknown opportunities and improved methods for executing tasks better and more rapidly. Consequently, the use of the Internet in finance, retailing, services and e-Business is changing the method business is transacted. Utilizing a knowledge-based system routine with improved technology introduces a new system of integrated processes and tools to help in defining new methods of problem solving and management. Data Mining can be applied in this phase, taking explicit knowledge found in databases and transforming it into useful knowledge.

The future of business lies in the process used to meet customer needs; detailed data and facts enhanced and critical awareness is transferred. GE Aircraft Engines for example, gets ahead of problems before they occur, diagnosing problems while monitoring aircraft engines during flight. By developing and stimulating their social networks GE is able to accomplish its work by locating and/or obtaining required replacement parts, compulsory resources or both, and have them on hand when the aircraft lands. The information assembled allows for reducing costs from lengthy engine repairs, and maintenance, resulting in increased efficiency and higher utilization of aircraft. Similar technology is now incorporated into medicine, utilities, automobiles, elevators, and an unknown number of other products, and directed to customer satisfaction.

The quest is in incorporating human capital into an emphasis on innovation and knowledge creation, while focusing on the collecting, accessing, leveraging and transferring of processes. Human capital may have emerged as the differentiating attribute for the 21st century workplace, but it is the worker's willingness combined with technology that provides the ability to access knowledge from the many sources desired in order to move forward.

Creation, the second phase, involves the organizing of the tacit knowledge captured and converting it into explicit forms such as words, concepts or other usable forms for analysis and understanding. *How* pertinent and valid the knowledge is, *what* is it worth, and *what* use will it be to the organization are questions to be answered. In essence, the system is concerned with more than just the processes that draws and stores knowledge into an organizational repository. It is crucial that the intellectual assets are organized in order to be harvested and used by others in support of solving problems and improving business judgments. The *Creation* process, when synthesized with the *Acquisition* process will result in the systemization, identification, structure and orderliness of identified knowledge so it can be retrieved easily. The outcomes are value-added efforts and improved operations since learning from experience becomes reality, proving that attained knowledge may be of greater significance than new learning. To insure the value of any human capital requires concentrating on internalizing all new and distinct knowledge, making it possible to amplify the various levels exponentially. Entering the creation process requires assessing the knowledge due to workforce personnel additions, and those who are leaving due to voluntary retirement or other reasons, who undoubtedly possess a wealth of skills and experience. In an atmosphere where knowledge has become a commodity, it is vital that prospering corporations have their intellect documented, and also know how to use it for advantage. Too often, when a successful initiative is completed, little or no documentation that might potentially assist others is unavailable.

Assimilation, the third phase in the cycle is where intellect deemed to be of merit is transferred, codified, integrated and applied by means of formal and informal processes and placed into a repository. This phase is a critical element to the system, as the relevance of the information presented is a major concern given that the decision to retain or reject any knowledge is conditional on its perceived relevance to the receiver. In the last process, *Dissemination,* technology is leveraged and human capital repositories consisting of acquired knowledge are made accessible for use in the development of new possibilities for economic and social returns including individual growth and development. The biggest problem confronting the harvesting of human capital is the dissemination of organizational knowledge, as it is not often known what is compulsory. An even greater problem may be the lack of systemic processes for the capture and transfer of this knowledge type.

Due to the lack of assessments organizations lose touch with employee attitudes and the intellect lacking. Consequently, managers are left with a handicap, because without this information they have no idea from *where* or *whom* this unknown can be located, and how to use and maintain the knowledge in its current state. Also, it is impossible to know how much has been lost given that it may not have been shared or documented, and can lead to poor judgment. The ideal system is not meant to replace current knowledge, but to assimilate it effectively and visibly to create synergy and meaning for the organization.

Consistency and repetition are two processes organizations want to continually realize. A person's ability to use organizational competencies effectively with consistency depends on establishing a standard of consistency in the workplace, which ultimately drives repeatability. McDonalds became successful as a result of the consistency of its operations process. Regardless of where their restaurants are geographically located, all of their processes are replicated. In fact, it is comical to go into a McDonald's at a time when there are no other customers and hear the server taking orders state in a loud voice, "*Next Please*." Nevertheless, it should be remembered that consistency is okay if the processes in place are respectable, but performing a task incorrectly or negatively can become a habit.

Although collaboration and cooperation are growing in importance, today's culture advocates that people strive to distinguish themselves as individuals. People will use and share knowledge if it is believed it will benefit them. An American Productivity and Quality Institute KMAT study determined 85% of companies surveyed believed their capability to manage knowledge was ineffectual. There are undoubtedly many reasons for this, but the most probable might be since knowledge is made up of intangibles, something that can't be managed. Yet, what can be managed is an environment where the knowledge can be created, captured, shared, leveraged, transferred and applied.

Human Capital Acquisition

Learning is a dynamic concept directed to the improvement of one's understanding, communications and ability to adapt to change. The real learning is obtained when determining who has what knowledge, being able to access it where it resides, and understand how it can be used. Accumulating an organization's human capital will not assure greater continuing substance, it requires commonality and should be able to alter the output and future action from the action observed in one's work processes.

The term *knowledge acquisition* has many synonyms, including knowledge elicitation, capture and gathering, implying a process involving first, the attainment, analysis, dissemination and structuring of knowledge from a variety of sources. Secondly, the sources for any acquisition efforts should include individual contributors, customers, suppliers and other stakeholders from within and outside the organization. The objective of the acquisition process is to first, systematically identify what knowledge is indispensable in satisfying the work processes performed. The process begins with determining, assembling and capturing the knowledge possessed by each source. The human capital is then analyzed to determine its usefulness to the organization's strategic objectives where the knowledge is codified and understood so it can be ordered and stored for effortless accessibility. The acquisition process then requires determining what criteria will be required for categorizing and grouping the knowledge captured. The process by which knowledge is attained contributes to the organizational repository where it is controlled for use, which is important that the personnel know how to use the knowledge in their work functions and, with it growing so rapidly the organization must be able to determine how to measure any basic variation. Knowledge attainment is possibly the most complicated of all aspects in the human capital process. Simply gathering an organization's human capital will not assure greater meaning since it should correlate to one's work processes and tasks for it to be of value. The biggest challenge comes in trying to control the many ad hoc groups that will be searching for particular information and knowledge.

In order for the information collected from an assessment to be recognized and offered for valid decision-making, it is essential that the information be reliable, systematic and inclusive. This requirement necessitates that any operation be evaluated without prejudice. Although there are many purposes for assessment, the central one is to determine how to turn human capital into effective action. This effort will require measures of learning key to building a knowledge aptitude and to proactively improve the process. It is critical that direct attention is paid to an employee's key knowledge and competencies of factual concepts within and outside of their work area. By determining the usefulness of an employee's knowledge and repeating the process, it is then possible to determine whether an organization is gaining or simply consuming this valuable asset.

A major criterion basic to the acquisition process is the standardization of the requirements desired. Standardization will increase the ability to identify and leverage the competencies of a workforce allowing for repeatability, reliability and consistency in providing valid outcomes. There are numerous methods for tapping into the strengths of individuals, such as; (1) interviewing techniques (addressing precise questions); (2) passive monitoring; (3) searching and extracting of e-mail files; (4) questionnaires, surveys or both; (5) portfolio assessments (describing step-by-step detailed processing and administrative behavior - the ISO requirements are an example); (6) building cases from problem-solving efforts; (7) video taping; (8) listening Posts; (9) action research (dialoguing about specific work operations); and (10) authentic assessments (observing of one's actions in addressing problems).

There are at least two schools of thought on how the organizations should determine the intellect level of an individual. The first, advocates the necessity of learning and the attainment of knowledge critical for staying might in the information age. Conversely, the second school does not believe it is possible to know what and the quantity of knowledge required. This is because of complications encountered in pulling together the knowledge desired, and deemed necessary for endurance; let alone its merit. In either case, having the ability to capture knowledge will result in one or more value-added repositories that will possess the skills, competencies and knowledge existing, within and outside of the organization. As the primary resource by which an organization's competitive advantage can be determined, it is critical the focus of human capital is on the indispensable knowledge, what is known, how much is possessed, and where it is located. A central focus is on the transfer and ability to navigate the knowledge repositories on hand, in addition to collecting knowledge from those who possess it. Methods such as surveys, interviews, and observations that convey how work is performed throughout the organization while reflecting on the tasks are some of the methods that can contribute to the accumulating of knowledge. It is also important to have an insight of what and how much human capital is bona fide, and to have a process to dispose of knowledge that is no longer valid in addition to determining the replenishment or augmentation of missing.

Human Capital: Leverage it or lose it

Although the industrial era gave rise to new business ventures and greater innovation it did not interact well with the situation, as it created problems requiring attention, such as Acid Rain, smog and global warming. Quite differently, the Information Era interacts strongly with both the market and the atmosphere, resulting in efforts requiring new rules.

Organizations have to focus on maintaining and creating relevant human capital, otherwise unknown amounts of knowledge will be lost, made unavailable or remain unarticulated. To a great extent the outcome of any knowledge loss in an organization is from not sharing and the loss of personnel. This comes from not knowing; who would benefit from particular knowledge; who has what knowledge, skills and competencies; how to share particular knowledge and finally, not understanding how the sharing of knowledge would help an individual and the organization. When asked about his failed experiments in developing the light bulb, Thomas Edison[2] stated that as a result, he knew 9,000 different ways of *how not* to make a light bulb. To Edison the experiments were not failures, but learning incidents, not just for himself, but for those working with him.

There are several key reasons why management would benefit from realizing *a know what they know* repository of knowledge. The first would satisfy the need to be able to do more with less, and second, it would help by means of the sharing and transferring of best practices out of leveraging and managing knowledge in their organizations. Leveraging experiences learned elsewhere can help in providing customers value-added products and services. This action provides the worker and organization greater strength and genuine understanding to act more effectively. A third reason is the need to direct attention to the increasing demand for improved customer service. Identifying the individuals who have greater knowledge will make it easier to prepare for the challenges in being customer-focused. The additional competencies determined to be possessed by the workforce will reduce the number of times knowledge must be re-created to satisfy a customer's request. Lastly, centers on the shortage of competencies in various settings, especially among high-tech companies. Identifying detailed competencies and resource requirements will make recruiting efforts more efficient, effective, quicker and less costly. The beginning location is at identifying and locating an organization's human capital and then matching these assets to its strategic initiatives. Vacancies filled more quickly help in moderating yield due to turnover.

Leveraging existing knowledge has become critical to sustaining an advantage. The ability to respond effectively is of greater importance if the tacit knowledge is obtainable to leverage by the teams, and/or groups of staff known as *Communities of Practice* (CoPs). CoPs occur everywhere, arising wherever workers function to address common, recurring problems, learning and sharing created knowledge. Informally united by proximity, common interest and purpose, a CoP's effort is to identify and solve common problems by engaging in sharing knowledge and experience. The end result is workers who are more capable in creating and applying greater levels of competence. CoPs are formally engaged in activities to do the right things more accurately and rapidly, often spanning organizational structures. As a small group – borrowing from Rosabeth Moss Kanter's[3] five F's - CoPs are able to *function* with greater *flexibility*, remain highly *focused*, are *friendlier* and enjoy themselves to the state having *fun*. The effect remains the same, developing meaning or purpose from the efforts of the community including the retaining of critical knowledge in the face of retirement and employee turnover. CoPs are usually successful and generate healthier outcomes than teams where the members constantly change because a compelling reason to exist is in place, and as a result develop implicit ways of working as one. Members of CoPs often become intuitively aware of what their teammates will do in given situations without necessarily communicating with one another. Wayne Gretsky, the famous star hockey player once stated his success was due to his ability to anticipate where his team-mates would direct the puck and going there to meet it. Nonetheless teams are usually unique and often less effective than CoPs as the purpose for existence is task driven, whereas CoPs are self-organized communities whose focus is directed to add value. An organization cannot force or create a CoP into existence, but it can seed, foster, support and encourage one in its alignment to satisfy its projects. The sharing process or methods addressed with CoPs can potentially benefit organizations across boundaries because of their utilization of human capital, possibly existing in various geographical locations. Micklethwaite[4] states, "A true learning organization is one in which knowledge ricochets around the system like a ball in a pinball machine." In other words, social networks need to be formed to shunt formal information from one end of the company to the other; moreover, barriers to unstated knowledge need to be discovered and removed. As such, it is possible to have a community of learning where individuals collaboratively share and learn from each other. Removing barriers that prevent individuals from engaging in collaborative activities through social relationships increases the dominance of community and sharing.

Human Capital Affect

A pedagogical problem challenging business today is determining how human capital might be used to help the workforce gain additional knowledge. Knowledge grows exponentially when shared among others, but may also present problems. How does an individual or an organization know when and if additional knowledge has been gained and what impact might it bring? Some argue that the same knowledge in a new distinct context becomes new knowledge created through the assimilation of what is known from new events and observations. Studies have indicated that about 80% of the potential human capital in an organization is unused and reveal that exhausting even a small amount of its intellectual resources can amount to an enormous loss. Having an awareness of who has what skills, competencies and proficiency would help in determining who should or should not be retained and retrained if necessary, should the situation be presented. Should it be the person with seniority who may have the greatest amount of human capital, or should it be the younger employee who might display greater energy and the possibility of being more innovative and creative, yet has less knowledge? These are questions easily answered if the correct information is on hand.

Having a wealth of human capital is not sufficient as organizations take on stewardship. Recognizing this untapped treasure and bringing it to the surface to leverage and make useable to others is a special task. It is not enough to just know what a person knows, or the way it is understood, since as humans they are always being shaped. The question becomes, of the local knowledge possessed what do we want shared and how accurate is it? The intent to share requires processes in place that will help in; (1) doing things more rapidly; (2) shrinking the process learning curve; (3) lowering the costs of operations; (4) supporting the performance of employees; (5) improving customer satisfaction; (6) leveraging best practices to hasten process improvement; and (7) being more innovative and creative. To satisfy these processes will require a reliance on the intent, the capital to be shared and the validity of functioning under a tradition, trusting and respecting what is amassed and stored.

Mission for Existence

Training has always been a controversial topic. Results of a published national survey[5], "The Other Shoe: Education's Contribution to the Productivity of Establishments," show a direct connection linking company profit and training investments. Studies show a link between employee operation enhancements and company profitability. Still others prove that using a systematic strategic technique to improving their employee's routine abilities will have greater profits and growth. The survey specifies a 10% increase in a worker's learning increased output from 8.6% to 11%, and investing in training in the non-manufacturing sector tripled productivity.

A second study[6] (1995) by the American Management Association (AMA) verified 45% of the companies surveyed that invested in training after restructuring or down-sizing encountered productivity improvements. During the same period over 42.8% of the companies that reduced training budgets saw production decline and almost 30% realized lower profits. After the John Deere Company cut spending for training and development, the company encountered enormous losses in the early 1990s, but after increasing their training and developing budget their human capital the company recognized a profit of over $400 Million in 1995 alone. Similar outcomes have been recognized by others, such as Toyota, Siemens and Motorola, who began monitoring ROI after training and development.

Rigorous training and development is crucial if a company is to keep pace with changing technology and remain competitive in a world marketplace. It has been proven that those investing in their human capital, working to develop, manage and retain valued employees hold the key to competitive advantage. Yet, training and development are often the first areas to experience budget cuts as management does not understand how learning can benefit a company in the long term. In contrast, corporations such as Siemens and Toyota, have spent millions on training and development in lieu of down-sizing, and have continually generated higher revenues, profits and earnings. At times being experienced currently in a down market is when companies should be training and developing their workforce in anticipation of the market improving.

Economic growth is based on the synergies between new knowledge and existing human capital, and explains why increases in training and education have supplemented major advances in technological sophistication in such countries as India and Ireland. These countries came to the realization that a competitive advantage could not be developed based simply on cheaper cost of labor. They determined that a continued investment in significant new resources in education or often re-education in developing qualified personnel would provide a significant factor in economic growth. The United States government appears to fail in recognizing that an improved quality of its workforce would have the greatest impact upon commerce. Although the demand for a highly skilled workforce is a variable element to increasing productivity, our government continues to dramatically reduce expenditures in education, training and development as experienced whenever problems with tax revenues are experienced.

If the essence of learning is to alter performance, organizations must encourage new behaviors that will help in improving each employee. This is only possible if the workforce's actions are aligned to the organization's strategic initiatives, necessitating effective measuring and knowing the competency differences of their human capital. Following this the organization must direct its efforts to their personnel development needs in order to close any performance gaps. or organizations to be flexible, innovative, growth oriented and responsive, new competencies are critical to produce desired behaviors. The problem is that the few companies measuring their workers are doing so against determined capabilities based on past or present performance and not to future needs, often looking at quantity versus the quality of talent.

Corporate Efficiency versus Human Costs

Human capital has become central to management responsibilities due to the new trends in business. These trends include the concern about personnel proficiency levels as a consequence of the lessening number of qualified recruits entering the workplace and the aging of the current workforce. This concern has presented a new conception of time, now a cultural life form. In recent years, corporations have come to realize that two thirds of their human resources will retire in a relative few years making the importance of eliciting and capturing their knowledge critical.

The increasing *rate of change,* another trend in the workplace presents a challenge to all aspects of concern because modification is a long-term endeavor for all organizations. The central variation threatening the work setting today is the fundamental demographic and ethical shifts reshaping how organizations regard expectations about life and work. Many have seemingly developed an attitude of complacency and even arrogance due to a belief that potential recruits possessing the mandatory human capital would be on hand when needed, and ignore developing those who might be retiring in a few years. In certain areas of business it is becoming more difficult to attract the more talented students, but an even greater problem is the continued lessening of workforce in the many areas such as Petroleum Engineering and Airline Pilots. These are area of study no longer appealing to students entering university. Consequently, some business areas will encounter severe workforce shortages in the future and will not have enough of the expertise, critical thinking skills and capabilities essential for up-and-coming jobs. Roger E. Herman[7] stated that the available pool of qualified workers is shrinking and will continue to do so late into the 21st century. He believes companies that can develop manage and retain its best and most knowledgeable personnel will have a decided advantage over its competitors. For this to be possible they must focus on the contribution individuals are capable of making, and be in tune with their needs and priorities. This unfortunately, appears to be only happening in smaller companies and not the more established ones.

Another trend, the c*ompetitive advantage,* is the result of making human capital central to management and the rising need to have the gusto and ability to remain ahead of the competition. This advantage comes from an organization's tacit knowledge giving it the ability to learn, collaborate, innovate and capitalize on its human capital more rapidly than its competitors. Every individual's role in the organization has to be examined in view of the fact that if prepared and accessible for possible later use, an individual's competence may be useful in an unknown number of situations.

Workforce mobility and reduction are often the outcome of an altered relationship involving the company and its personnel. The mobility rate of the experienced professional is in the order of 40% and their leaving is often unplanned, unexpected and expensive to replace. When independent people leave, precious human capital, relationships and the vitality needed to pursue innovation and creativity is diminished. Mobility is a major business issue today and one crucial to competitive advantage as continual turnover affects strategic initiatives by inhibiting processes and interrupting progress.

Evidence suggests that whenever a new managerial line of attack or philosophy for doing business is introduced many in the environment follow suit. It is not until some implementers experience success deploying the attitude does the particular practice become accepted, popular and deployed by other companies. This was experienced with such methodologies as MBO, TQM, Re-engineering, and Six Sigma. This does not imply however, that any new practice is beneficial to all organizations. Down-sizing, outsourcing, re-organizing and reengineering are examples of managerial methodologies that have spread throughout the business communities with an outcome that regrettably may not have been the one desired. They are often an excuse, a reactive effect to address a mistake that upper management made that comes back to bite them and their impact contribute to the: (1) discrepancy of skills and competencies; (2) workload disparity for the remaining workforce; (3) reduced investment in the workforce; (4) succession planning questions; and (5) lack of strategic planning. Unfortunately, these processes have turned into a march similar to Sherman's and all areas of business, the workforce, family members and the communities have seemingly been affected negatively as a result of these methodologies.

The strong traditions of paternalism dominating corporate life from the 1940s through the 1970s have all but disappeared. The values-based thinking and belief of how human resources should be treated, once promoted by such corporations as IBM, GE, Ford, and Procter & Gamble no longer exists. Corporations once believed to be advancing the American way of life by means of more and better jobs at higher wages are now eliminating or slashing the workforce in a merciless and profound manner with seemingly no concern. The ruthless, restructuring methods used has developed a feeling of mistrust in the workplace. Concern for improving bottom-line results in the short-term has replaced values-based thinking. The only benefactors appear to be the senior executives who are seemingly rewarded with huge reparation packages for reducing the workforce they were often responsible for building initially. While some of the increase might be the upshot of the perception (right or wrong) that fat was getting cut, in many instances when workers are cut, costs decrease and as a consequence, earnings increase, at least temporarily. Often, layoffs are credited to short-term increases in stock market prices, resulting in senior executives' enormous remuneration. Research on the other hand, has shown the majority of firms using the layoff tactic ultimately ended with stock prices below the pre-layoff price. This suggests that the short-term euphoria of cost cutting is eventually followed by the sobering recognition that when personnel costs are reduced, so too are the assets that generate future revenue and profitability. It has been determined that voluntary attrition programs have often targeted the more valuable experienced workers who take their informal social network with them, making the loss of institutional memory even greater. Morgan Stanley compensated CEO Phil Purcell $66 Million, then suffered a 25% decline in stock prices and while Computer Associates paid its CEO $655 Million in 1999 the company saw its stock price fall 72% in 2000. More examples are Richard Fuld, who had been paid $354 Million over five years and as CEO of Lehman Brothers forced the company as the largest in times past to bankruptcy. Stanley O'Neal left Merrill Lynch with a package worth $160 Million and then in less than a year the investment house was forced into a takeover by Bank of America. His replacement Thain was given a $15 Million signing bonus and after three quarters of extreme loses felt he should be awarded a $10 Million bonus. Ken Thompson was ousted from Wachovia and awarded a golden parachute worth over $5 Million, Chuck Prince was forced out at Citigroup and given a parting gift valued at $16 Million, and more recently the CEO of Washington Mutual received $18 Million for three weeks of work before it was taken over by J.P. Morgan Chase. It hasn't ended there however, as stated in a Forbes magazine article "Bonuses" 02/19/09 Wall Street executives of financial institutions that received stimulus funds from the government shared over $18 Billion in bonuses in 2008. All of these excessive senior management compensation packages and worker reductions have prompted mistrust in the workplace.

Although still employed, many workers believe they have lost the security they may have once had. These are often loyal long-term personnel who made sacrifices over the years and expected the company to remember their loyalty during difficult periods. Companies have been subjected to decreased efficiency given that key people randomly lost are often those who are older, more knowledgeable, and higher-compensated. Those remaining, untouched by the attenuation, often waste a good amount of their work day discussing potential job losses instead of working. Regardless of the atmosphere though, self-interest cannot sustain the workers for long. Management must work to harness possible collective energy in the pursuit of corporate goals and values, but must also help the worker in possessing a context, a sense of self-worth, and an identity. If addressed properly this could develop into an opportunity to create a new and improved corporate culture and ultimately result in a competitive advantage.

Eventually, because of the reduction efforts, many organizations develop a greater awareness of the intellectual worth residing in the heads and interactions of their employees. When this awareness comes to light it develops value as both corporate human capital and a source for competitive advantage, but as the amount and depth increases, it is essential that it be captured, stored, and made accessible for future use.

Organizational Learning

In her book Zuboff[8] writes "Learning is no longer a separate activity that occurs either before one enters the workplace or in remote classroom settings . . . learning is the heart of productive activity . . . the new form of labor." It would be quite impossible to discuss how a company could or should benefit from its human capital without first discussing organizational learning, a continuous spiral, requiring information, facts and data where knowledge is dispersed to greater productive capability. The ultimate outcome in using this asset is an improvement in the capacity for change, innovativeness and effectiveness based on the human capital brought forward. Consequently, changes can be predicted and revisions to the organization's strategy made in a timely manner. Having the ability to adopt break-through technologies more rapidly than the competition means the development and constant upgrading of the strategic and proprietary competencies will be experienced.

Garvin[9] notes that for organizational learning to be successful three overlapping stages contribute to the enabling, managing, leveraging and re-use of knowledge. The first, the *Cognitive* stage, combines new knowledge obtained from effective learning and prior knowledge enhancing new methods to solve problems by creating new and expanding knowledge. In the second, the *Behavioral* stage, individuals alter established patterns by internalizing new insights. This stage may include the recruiting of new personnel, developing new relationships, and collaborating with those outside of the organization. Embodying human capital through acquisitions can bring about; improved communications, unique insights, the collaboration of efforts over competing, and innovative products and services. Lastly, the *Performance* stage, brings measurable improvement, which can be observed and verified. Bringing a substitute player from the bench into a basketball game for example, demonstrates how learning is best arrived at by means of socialization where organizational composition can assist relationships. On a basketball team, each player has complimentary skills. Taken separately these skills do not add up to a complete team, but if used wisely, each player's capabilities can balance one another for healthier results. Each of a worker's human capital assets has its own character and if allowed will contribute to an effective end result for the organization, and by expanding the ability of each individual the organization's will also. This is only possible by way of continually enhancing the interdependent relationships from an organization's distributed sources.

Learning has greater results when directed to satisfying an organization's resourcefulness if the workforce is provided opportunities for greater knowledge-intensive capability development. It has been proven learning is enhanced and the usefulness of skills greater when a network of interpersonal connections and infrastructures is involved. Although competitors, Toyota and GM have proven it is possible to collaborate and operate in new markets. These two corporations gained an enormous amount of awareness from their partnership at the California based New United Motor Manufacturing Company, Inc. (NUMMI). Toyota learned about American workers, Human Capital and markets, while GM learned about Japanese management methods, such as group concepts. Toyota put their newly developed understanding to greater quality use when building its own manufacturing facilities in the United States, and GM benefited from their new learning in developing its innovational Saturn facility in Tennessee. This is interesting as Toyota has been grown to obtain huge success in the auto industry while GM is on the verge of bankruptcy.

It does nothing to have human capital if it cannot be transferred throughout the organization quickly. Many managers and individual contributors may grumble about the situation, but many still reluctantly address the situation. When fear becomes entrenched in the workplace, the workers will not complain openly, as they value their jobs and are afraid of losing them. Therefore, workers are reluctant to speak up and share, limiting creativity. It has been estimated that only 10 % of an organization's human capital, is employed daily. The estimated amount may be greater or less with some, but through better explicit management of their human capital business problems could be diminished. Human capital can be used for unfair, fraudulent and even dangerous means, an unfortunate, but not a universal rule.

Controls are critical to insure the knowledge user is never placed into a questionable situation, but as stated there appears to have been a lack of direction and identified controls with many companies. A great deal has been written about the need for improved business controls and incentives as possible solutions. Examining the process honestly would likely indicate a lack of understanding of the method by which organizational human capital is managed and would likely prove to be the central reason for business failures. Having a strong corporate society where employees are supported and provided direction might have reduced situations that occurred with such companies as: Barings Securities, Snapple/Quaker Oats, Tyco, Enron Corporation, Arthur Anderson, WorldCom, Yamaichi Securities and others.

Computers are incredibly fast, accurate, and stupid;
humans are incredibly slow, inaccurate, and brilliant;
together they are powerful beyond imagination.
Albert Einstein[1]

Chapter 4

Technological Advancement and Human Interaction

In today's explosive setting technology is no longer simply a company resource; it is a mode of life. Companies see themselves, trapped in a vicious cycle; attempting to meet the challenges for survival and opportunities for prosperity. Until recently, the focus of information technology was on explicit knowledge directed to decreasing what could be captured and transferred to where it should be directed. Although intended to assist the efficient eliciting and storing of undocumented information, there is still uncertainty as to technology's contribution to effectiveness. What has come about is an event now known as the productivity paradox; the result of companies investing in technology, but not being able to recognize any benefits. The reason for this is that new technologies do not guarantee the workers will alter their mode of operation. Technology should make it possible to locate the requisite information and knowledge, and determine how it is linked in order to be accessed in order that it can be used for increased productivity. Although few people are aware of how technology works, its direction must be directed to increase yield by adding value in the form of knowledge and competence. Today, most work is performed by utilizing the information centered on the accessibility of unspoken knowledge in the course of repetitive collaborative experiences. By way of the use of new tools, people-to-people, organization-to-organization, location-to-location and network-to-network interactions have become possible. Still new strategic thinking focusing on assorted methods directed to satisfying the needs and expectations of customers, and creating customer value will be essential to thrive. All are made possible by eliminating time and space as constraints to the application of knowledge while replacing them with computers and networks.

Then again, measuring the effect of technology to business, carrying out and taking responsibility for the creation and use of knowledge repositories in improving performance, is not sufficient. Doing things as always is not adequate, but by means of technology, processes can be examined to determine how to influence them.

Often costs removed from a company's expense base are often re-introduced in an attempt to satisfy a short-term effort. Since labor makes up most of an organization's costs this is the first area reduced in hopes of making up any shortfall. Nevertheless it is those let go that are often the key organizational figures vital for durable growth. At one time, managers may have believed technology would enhance productivity, but technology does not necessarily make workers more productive. Productivity gains are an outcome of what individuals do by means of technology, not by just having it. To increase productivity requires that workers continually learn new technologies while working.

Having technical familiarity will help make an individual more valuable, capable and competent because with greater familiarity execution will improve. Working together will help the organization go beyond improving it's functioning and strengthening its advantage. Sejersted[2] suggests that technology is a cultural and social product adapted as a force reflecting a person's daily life. Since the 1980's, technology has transformed the manner business is performed. It is beginning to support the social relationships concerning people since this is where the significance of knowledge exchange through collaboration is generating. Through the introduction of Lap-tops, fax machines, e-mail, voice-mail, cellular phones, chat rooms, instant messaging, blogs, Wikis and other communication means, it is not difficult to see how when combined with an individual's extended workload, valuable time can be taken and or lost to these media.

As stated, an organization can have even greater might if it can access the human capital of its workers, regardless of location. In so doing, two aspects are judged: (1) technology affecting all levels of the organization; and (2) the human mind processing knowledge differently from the technology used. Because of these aspects, organizations require greater involvement when helping workers to be better users of the technology to perform their responsibilities. If this relationship does not exist, both the organization and the workforce will be short-lived. One area requiring attention involves a movement to having the employees work remote, usually from home. Working at home requires discipline, a definite adjustment in attitude, conduct and a special thought process and as a result, both management and the worker need to think differently in order to understand and direct attention to today's operating tribulations.

New technology has seldom lowered cost. The highest costs result from the human element given that it is people who are indispensable in making the adjustments, modifications or both as required. The technological skills desirable are complicated, requiring qualified high-tech workers who are difficult to acquire and as a result generates higher salaries. This requirement has stimulated a number of questions. How do organizations: (1) acquire the skills and competencies required to reflect the changes confronting them if they are not readily presented? (2) obtain enhanced meaning out of their technological competencies? (3) implement a process that will measure and ensure a continual bringing up to date of the skills and competencies needed? (4) prove a value is provided? It is therefore, crucial to determine if the questions asked are respectable and have an understanding of the particular technological operations insinuated by the questions. The biggest question is will the knowledgeable individuals crucial in satisfying the desired outcomes be open to answer them?

Although suited for the storage and transfer of explicit knowledge, little is known about how technology can be used for its elicitation, capture, creation, and sharing. Throughout recorded history, technology has been the drive responsible for change in unpredictable ways. In today's setting for example, the need for knowledge technology has become evident in the areas of distance learning, process management and collaborative systems.

New opportunities have come about as a result of technology and disproportionate amounts of value can be expected in the future, often the consequence of efforts to improve current methods. These new opportunities may provide the users direct access to the indispensable knowledge sources. Collaboration, in turn, becomes harder due to limitations such as one's ability to perceive what others see, understand and are doing. Unaided, technology might not contribute to the immediate benefit of society, because making modifications to knowledge in a collaborative mode requires something other than technology: it involves an alteration in conduct.

As a defining characteristic, technology has laid the foundation for growth in future opportunities, but simply understanding technology does little to prepare workers during periods of radical adjustment however, being flexible and aggressive does. In today's emergent economy, where skills and knowledge are quickly outmoded, regardless of where or what is done, technology has become a major facet in all efforts. Technology can still create upheaval while directing to the worker's actions and influencing their work if it is not directed to adapt to the learner's slant. Where human capital involves the elicitation, capture, retrieval, storage and communication, technology is the tool used to assist with these functions.

The 21st century labor force is still attempting to understand the technology of the Information Era, but what was supposed to give them greater freedom may have become a curse. Workers often feel they are slaves to technology and have difficulty prioritizing or recognizing the difference between the urgent and less significant activities to be performed. While driven to do more, workers worry about losing their jobs and work extended hours. Until the economic downturn, Americans had been working over 2200 hours a year, 200 more than their closest rival, the Japanese, and 500 hours more than the Europeans. This has increased even more in the last year. These hours are usually the additional time an employee spends at the office or working at home to complete work in process. The fear of out of sight, out of mind, appears to be a factor. Many workers believe that if management does not see them they might believe they are not needed. Ultimately, workers generate less quality work and personally experience a poorer quality of life. Research points out that only 14% of the U.S. workforce takes a two week vacation. It is believed that this extended work may contribute to workers suffering "*Burnout,*" the state of stress, contributing to exhaustion, a loss of energy and frustration. This accumulation of chronic stress may contribute to less motivated workers, who dislike and may even hate their job. Therefore, they are less productive and if possible may even leave. The rapid and extensive pace in an unpredictable milieu has placed an emphasis on working feverishly to learn how to transform and improve business strategies and operational efficiencies. This effort is performed while intensifying innovation and speed to meet market response, and will require an understanding of the organization's goals, helping the workers develop, understand and sharing the value of human capital. Putting it all together will require a new way of life based on mutual support, enthusiasm, admiration and appreciation for each person's contribution.

A new emphasis in technology today is digitization, an effort meant to generate unlimited efficiency by means of less human labor at a time when a shortage of skilled labor exists. The introduction of digitization has nevertheless, not only helped in trimming down manpower in all areas of corporations today, it is actually helping personnel work themselves out of a job. For example, airlines, hotels and auto rental companies use the internet to make reservations, having the customer doing all the work, allowing the workforce to be trimmed down. This is an interesting predicament; presented when management is looking for their human resources to be highly innovative, collaboration and productive. It is difficult to believe these efforts can be realistic when the stress and worry about losing one's job can have a major affect on productivity. In some cases, those let go may be the ones who created the technology being used and often not recognized for their efforts. Yet, through the advent of the Internet, management's desire for a workerless environment may be getting closer to reality. Digitization has made it possible for the knowledge that once existed or exists in the heads of the workers to be made obtainable to anyone, anywhere, communicating on-line in various languages by way of little or no supervision or intervention.

Technology as a Tool

Technology has been with us for some time and its rate of change continues to gather speed. It helped enable the move from the *Agrarian Age,* which began around 1840 by means of mechanical devices using kinetic energy, lasting almost 60 years to the beginning of the *Industrial Age* in the 1920's. Prior to the *Industrial Age*, knowledge was applied to tools and technology at what may have seemed a snail's pace. History has shown that years seem to pass before conversion is widespread enough to affect large numbers; the introduction of the printing press is recognized as the first. Although humans create and generate knowledge, technology has become critical to human capital as it has become the main driver of an organization's resources. It is for this reason that it can alter the course workers think about and perform in their jobs. Utilizing human capital effectively creates value with, rather than simply delivering it, and technology is a tool that can be employed to connect people sharing their knowledge. As a tool, technology plays a significant role in effective knowledge sharing because of today's global aspects. Technology must help workers function in new and value-added ways providing a means of storing intelligent information versus just data, while at the same time help in acquiring and developing new products and services. Using Personal Computers and communicating via e-mail, Sametime, Chat-rooms, Skype, Blogs, Fax, cellular phones, video-conferencing and telecommuting, technology allows professionals the resources required to prepare their own correspondence, presentation development etc., thereby eliminating the need for administrative assistance. Technology is often assigned too much authority and acts as though all things should work for it instead of it working for the worker. As an example, the technological capability can consume time when searching for unnecessary information and knowledge. When researching a particular topic, the worker may discover areas of greater interest and branch out to locate information that may or may not be applicable.

Technology has become difficult to ignore. In today's setting, as the pace of adjustment increases in the pursuit to improving operations, knowledge is generated from multiple areas, but given that businesses function in operational silos where interests focus on one part of the organization and not the whole. As a result, the generation of sharing and new knowledge creation is hindered due to the workforce's inability to adapt fast enough, the increase in worker mobility and the frowning ofknowledge sharing and informal networks. Through its ability to locate information, technology has moved to where brainpower rather than horsepower has become the determining factor for success. Synergizing brainpower and technology in a fast and innovative manner allows organizations to grow, because workers are able to work more rapidly, due to added effectiveness and efficiency. Although technology allows even the less knowledgeable to access volumes of intelligence to make improved decisions, advanced skill and proficiency levels are crucial if an individual desires to look into something with greater depth.

Although becoming a vital resource, technology brings consequences. Eliminating the need to compete in an area of business can introduce problems never before contemplated. As an example, E-Business may not be the decisive answer, as it could force out the competition by eliminating suppliers for a desired product or service. Another problem might be with companies working to digitize themselves when potential consumers have neither the capability to access nor the desire to transact business in an electronic format. As a rule, consumers prefer convenience, but even more prefer to choose the manner business is performed and may even rebel against those insisting on an alternate method. Companies sometime forget that the older population, those who possess the majority of the disposable money have not all accepted the e-business' method of transacting business.

Certainly, innovative methods of processing information need to be identified, but it is of greater value if the criteria placed on those involved is known and understood. Through the introduction of the printing press information was easily disseminated to the general public, and the Internet has proven capable of providing additional ability sooner to even more people. Yet, knowledge accessible more rapidly at lower costs is not necessarily free, something evident with some consumers having to conduct business via the internet. There are many people in the world who still do not have the means to own a computer and are unable to access the benefits possible. As an example, some airlines will only accept reservations via the internet and charge a fee if the reservation is made via the telephone along with higher fares. Instead of excluding a body of potential customers, I believe companies should work to identify new and innovative methods to retain and achieve business with all of their customers, while attracting still others. These companies appear to forget it is a lot cheaper to keep a customer than to attract a new one.

Today, no method for providing ultimate customer service via the internet is possible. Companies competing in this economy have difficulty overcoming the social challenges needed in addressing customer needs and expectations in providing customer service. An especially critical problem involves the United States losing supremacy as the world's technological leader to such countries as Germany and Japan. This loss has occurred in many areas of technology such as, computers, telecommunications, electronics and semiconductors. Nevertheless the problem does not end there. Issues such as accessibility and connectivity in less than 30% of the homes in the United States (where most of the Internet users reside) have high-speed communications connectivity as compared to 97% of the homes in Singapore are evident. In fact, according to the Organization for Economic Co-operation and Development (OECD) the U.S. continues to fall behind and is now considered in 20th place in broadband internet penetration, right after Luxembourg. It doesn't end there however. The high-speed Internet access in the U.S. is considerably slower than most other countries. The median download speed is less than 2.0 megabits in contrast to Japan is at 61 mbps, South Korea's at 45 mbps, France's at 17 mbps and Canada's at 7 mbps. Although this is changing with wireless capabilities made more available, in weighing against other countries, the U.S., the country where the process started is falling behind. If organizations are to continue changing, better-quality, faster, cheaper and improved communications connectivity will be necessary along with additional knowledgeable people. This is possible by integrating technologies, which will allow work groups to learn and share knowledge. Being able to access information has no definite advantage unless people can add significance and transform information to knowledge, to be leveraged and shared.

Accessing Repositories

An issue of vital importance is possibly society's growing dependency on the Internet to satisfy its informational needs. Designed by the Department of Defense in the 1980's to exchange information the Internet has led to many improvements in the last twenty five years, but it is also causing many companies to bend under the weight of enormous amounts of information. Where it was once believed imperative to have large amounts, today's emphasis is on workers having access to the right information in the right format, at the right time, all at the proper quality level desired. Since technology is a force based on awareness, those with greater technical knowledge may temporarily wield greater strength.

Given that changes come so quickly, it is often not known what to do next. There is no set of metrics, and/or common definitions identified, and little understanding existing for use in implementing and developing any of them. The outcome is often an inability to integrate technology effectively with consistency in order to collect, store and access the human capital available. Because technology is meant to influence all aspects of the corporation, each area will feel whatever affects the others. Some believe technology is meant to provide new and innovative ways of competing. Actually, the purpose of technology should be to provide closer collaborative methods that can help influence organizational human capital in the development and implementation of high-quality products and personalized service.

Even if the technological architecture exists, human capital is never found in only one location and is often in assorted formats. While today's storage media is suited for storing and conveying large volumes of explicit information, there is a limit to the number of applications to be had dealing with the transfer and exchange of the collective human capital of the workforce. The storage media available vary with the location of the workers. It can be computer media, (CDs, diskettes), to the contents of desk drawers, journals, file-cabinets and boxes in warehouses all reflecting a fraction of what is known. Accessing information in a common format is near impossible and the processes essential to accomplish this requires specialized expertise, necessitating the continued development of the personnel. Companies maintain a multitude of countless databases, some referred to as *Knowledge Centers,* which store data and information usually captured for other purposes. In many instances, these databases contain similar or duplicated information not easily accessible by other organizations or have significant differences that must be addressed before the desired information can be used. In addition, the understood information, which should be collected on top of experiences, is seldom saved. These knowledge centers are meant to help with the compilation, orderliness and dissemination of particular information.

Owing to the shift from time-honored to contemporary, new technology is typified by several key modifications, such as the need and use of skilled personnel. In focusing attention to this adjustment and to function effectively in a technological milieu all employees require a core employability ability at all levels. No one disagrees that the improvement of business performance and productivity in support of strategic initiatives requires technology. Like all schemes, human capital concepts and information technology are necessary, and must be included in the process through all phases of implementation and involvement. As a result, today's technological professional is required to think and work uniquely.

Today, depending on how technology is used, life can be made easier by way of improved working conditions and a productive labor force. No longer do we have to consider ourselves remote. By utilizing the proper technology companies have the ability to produce something with others in a joint effort across borders and cultures regardless of location. It is possible to send a document to someone in Paris while an individual in Japan updates a spreadsheet addendum, and still another person in New York appends a drawing to the document; all communicating with an individual situated in a remote area of Colorado, who receives the revisions concurrently. Technological capabilities may have eliminated the geographical distance barriers, but the creativity and innovativeness is in determining how to accomplish extra by means of fewer resources. This effort requires the competencies, motivation and the capacity for continual learning. This necessitates a system where workers are exposed to the collecting, creating, understanding and storing of knowledge in a repository whose contents can then be leveraged and shared in order to influence the surroundings where we operate.

Time is of the Essence

Management is obliged to accept accountability for the ongoing and post assessments that determine firm success resulting from the transition of what has occurred after any development and what might happen lacking it. This interaction requires an understanding that will assimilate information in addition to the delicate characteristics motivating each employee into action. Knowing '*Why*' something happens the way it does will help this process. As vital as it is for having the employees involved in the process, it is even more important that the information determined from any assessment be reported and shared through the entire concern. A potential problem in reporting the information is its complexity, misunderstanding and misuse by those who might have access to said information. Controls are essential to insure no misuse of the information, something necessary when a trusting relationship does not exist.

When considering strategy as a military topic, we can think of a repository of human capital as a weapon in an organization's war chest. In *The Five Rings,* Musashi[3] states all weapons have a distinctive spirit. The distinctive spirit of human capital may well be *time*. An organization's human capital is created, captured, accumulated and maintained in a model referred to as the "Intellectual Capital Determination System." I believe this can be illustrated by utilizing a process introduced by Deming as his Plan-Do-Check-Act (PDCA) cycle (Figure 6).

The *Plan* phase, which should be directed by management, can be referred to as the strategic management process. In this process management clarifies, details and establishes an integrated system of strategic planning to manage their talent. The managers reveal the direction the company should take toward achieving stated identifiable plans. It is vital that management ensures each person is moving in the same direction, and they have the determined business-driven skills and competencies. This process may call for establishing a training and development program for the continual learning, retooling and re-skilling of its personnel. In satisfying the need for a skilled workforce it is compulsory to design all training and development with the technology, setting and knowledge-dissemination basic practices to support collaboration and teamwork.

The *Do* phase determines the level of intellect identifying where it exists, to what extent is valid, and it's standing in relationship to the competition. Determining all of this information is middle management's responsibility. It is a practice seldom performed, as intangible assets are often regarded as soft information with little significance or meaning. In most cases, employees are assessed on output, not the methods used to perform their work. In this strength of mind process, the organization correlates the human capital essential against that possessed by each worker to determine the company's capabilities in order to remain competitive. If this process is to thrive managers must know their; (1) key processes; (2) inputs (resources used) to the processes and the outputs (products, services or both); (3) customers who purchase these products or services and; (4) expected outcome for each of the processes.

The *Check* phase realizes the capability assessments and evaluations of the workforce's intellect-level with its training and development needs. The measures should be directed to clear-cut, useful, and realistic operations while identifying problems that require correction if value-added outcomes are to be generated. This can be seen in a Toyota automotive plant where the workers will stop the assembly line whenever a defect is identified so it can be corrected preventing the possibility of repetition. Management functions as coaches and mentors, imparting open and credible feedback during the development process. This is contrast to the big three, GM, Ford, and Chrysler where stopping the line is frowned upon and corrections to problems are resolved after the automobile is completely assembled, often by the dealer.

PDSA CYCLE

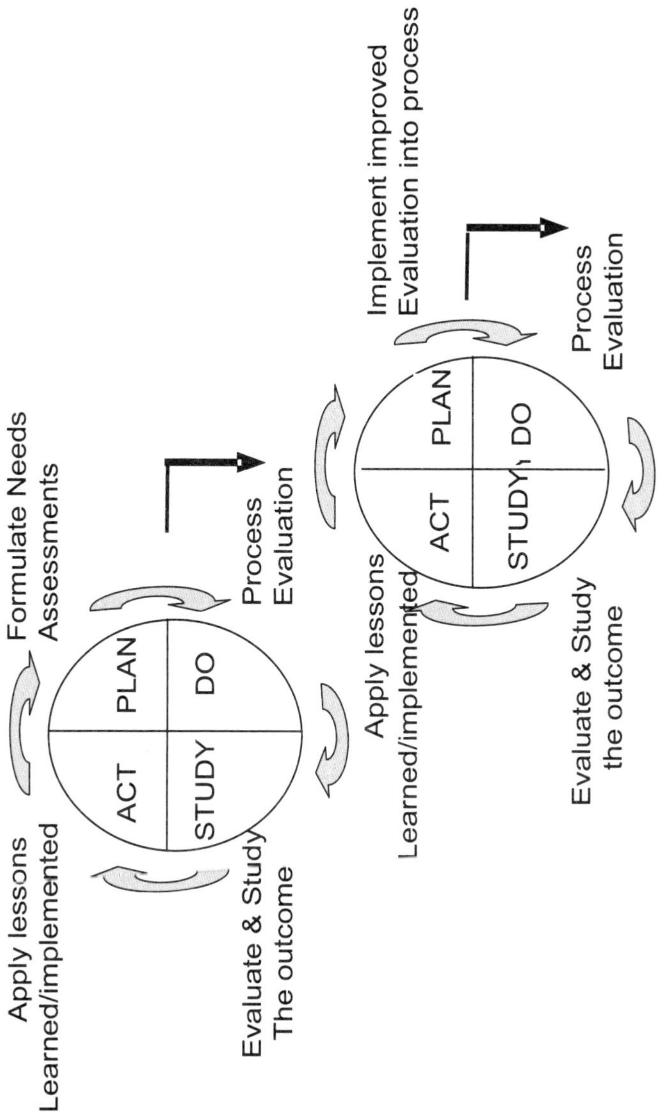

Figure 6

Finally, in the *Act* phase the organization identifies how it will deal through corrective action and the adjustments needed in achieving its objectives. This phase determines where the recent human capital created is to be applied in order to arrive at superior end results. Business leaders and employees are beginning to realize their jobs cannot be maintained consistently. Nevertheless, there are some who seem to believe the skills required in today's workplace will be the same through the 21st century workplace. To ensure the capability of addressing its needs will require an understanding and analysis of what learning each employee should have. In so doing, management needs to consider the following questions are asked:

- What business needs are to be satisfied?
- What desired skill levels should the organization have?
- What are the critical areas that will generate problems?

Knowledge Repositories and Navigation

Discovery becomes a fundamental aspect of any knowledge system effort, and this process should allow for the locating, eliciting, mining and accessing of the human capital inside an organization. An organization's knowledge repository is the accumulation of known information, experiences, skills and competencies validated by each member. To be of value it is essential that the contents of all individual repositories are networked in order to exploit the existing human capital. Having access to the knowledge makes development highly systematic and helps workers do what they do best more quickly.

In order to do so management must be able to link the distinct formidable knowledge repositories in the workplace, and leverage them into an informational system where they can be accessed as required. Allowing for ease and accessibility of learning the outcome will be enhanced learning and understanding. To maintain the knowledge stored, it is crucial information about future technologies, writings on emerging developments, trends, forecasts and research be included. In turn, newly discovered or created knowledge has to be assimilated into a format where outdated knowledge can be managed and removed in a timely fashion. Repositories have been built in order to store large amounts of data, yet the knowledge essential to know what to do by way of the data and information collected is seldom stored, and consequently it is difficult to manage in a self-renewing method. If organizations were aware of and have access to their human capital, they could address it more effectively, adding value and ultimately result in a level of improved efficiency and greater competitive advantage. Organizations have always had practice in managing data and information, but little with knowledge, something of no usefulness until it is captured and leveraged for benefit.

Organizations need to shift their focus from developing workers in explicit technologies to developing them in distinctive competencies. Working collaboratively across the distributed sources and having access to a repository of particular capabilities, skills and knowledge is a major facet of aggressive action as it improves the effectiveness of management and problem solving. This knowledge repository should consist of applied competencies and or technical expertise, or operational capabilities and the requirements needed to satisfy a particular job function. These are the strategic capabilities that help distinguish superior performance; the root essentials of a company's or an individual's expertise; and the special attributes or behavioral skills that identify how employees act and function, working to provide a company a competitive advantage.

As new commanding technologies are introduced, it will be possible to improve automation and offer larger storage capacity with quicker access. Continual amendments make integrating and managing the repositories and their contents a problem. To resolve these problems additional personnel will be required to examine, evaluate, structure and disseminate information so it can be used and directed to providing a business advantage. To do well, decision-making systems should dictate how human capital in the correct format is made available to meet broader and more complex business needs.

Financial Business Aspects

David Bernoulli[4] (c.1798) introduced the concept of human capital as the so-called thrust in economic growth, and defined wealth as "anything that can contribute to the adequate satisfaction of any sort of want." Bernoulli believed a process would be essential to govern the value-added method of utilizing the sum of one's formal and informal education, talent, and competencies. In his St. Petersburg paper, Daniel Bernoulli, a mathematician, stated that "... expected values are computed by multiplying each possible gain by the number of ways in which it can occur, and then dividing the sum of these products by the total number of cases." The idea behind his statement is that the greater the knowledge an individual possesses, the less their additional learning will be evaluated. An individual's intellectual assets can then be accessible and shared as a high-level collection of organizational knowledge through a process known as "*Knowledge Warehousing*." Through a serious emphasis on openness an individual using shared effort and human capital stored in a repository would be able to achieve greater productivity, make things faster, cheaper and with better-quality than if functioning alone. This process will allow for the replicating of business awareness into other areas, greatly multiplying the effects.

The three identified functions center on the human capital aspect of a company's intellectual asset base and identify the areas where management should direct its attention as in

Figure 7. In so doing, it is critical that management determines and develops an inventory of the workforce's competencies, and capabilities that require further development or need to be obtained.

Intellectual Asset Base

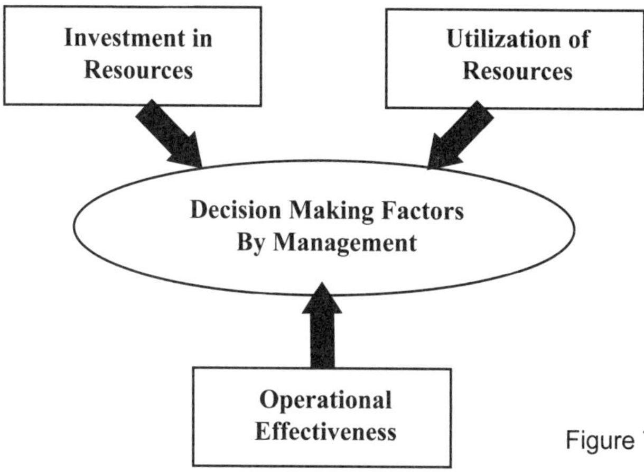

Figure 7

Although companies admit the value of human capital, fewer than 30% of them have measures in place to determine the effectiveness of their human capital assets on business impact. I believe the absence of measurement is alarming and contributes to a lack of understanding on how to alter the workforce's performance by giving the workers the time and attention deserved.

Traditional accounting has paid little attention to human capital. Unlike all other factors of production workers cognition is more difficult to measure and cannot be owned and has an indefinite service life. Things are changing how-ever, as new methods are examined and introduced to include intellectual assets in the same way as those that are tangible. It goes beyond simply examining and knowing a worker's worth in an economic sense it needs to transform the usefulness from the employee's contribution into an organization's capability. Since there is still no set body of rules to support the estimating and reporting of the cumulative aspects of intangibles, addressing a worker's human capital may lead to a number of moral and ethical questions. There are many skeptics who doubt that something which does not physically change hands can be measured. They differ from those who look for methods of measurement instead of how human capital can be used as a distinctive advantage. As a consequence of the major restructuring of the 1980s and into the 1990s, massive layoffs were generated, and corporations typically enjoyed dramatic increases in their stock prices. Undoubtedly the effect of the perception (right or wrong) that fat was getting eliminated. Some of the increases in stock price may have been simply because when labor is cut, costs are reduced. Research has shown the majority of firms that used the layoff tactic eventually experienced stock prices below the pre-layoff price. This suggests the short-term elation of cost cutting is eventually followed by the recognition that when worker costs are cut, the assets generating future revenue and profitability are also. What is mandatory therefore, when there is a reference to human capital, is a measurement process to develop a value determination for what is meant to various workgroups, teams and organizations.

Assigning an explicit financial worth to intangibles is complex since people tapping the knowledge possessed through learning and interacting with others brings variation to an individual's competency interactions. The appropriate action varies with the work to be performed, relationships with distributed sources and persons external to the areas involved. It is essential that learning opportunities are systematic and planned to provide personnel the compulsory competencies and opportunities to learn and use. These opportunities should have clear-cut standards that deal with accessing, instructions and connections, plus best practices. In achieving the needed standards, it is essential to redirect the focus from training in explicit technologies to developing competencies to a wider range of expertise. Possessing competencies implies proficiency in multiple skills and provides a vehicle by which new learning can be adopted as required to increase production. If only trained in technical tools there is little for the employee to build on when the tools become outdated. As technology becomes embedded in the business process, mandatory understanding converts from one of specialization to one of generalization. This switch implies requiring a significant depth of awareness and expertise in a particular discipline combined with a limited range of learning in other disciplines. In contrast, it is crucial to have a broad-breadth of familiarity in a multitude of disciplines, but not having much depth and de-emphasizing specialization might be a greater advantage to the manner business is performed.

In their pursuit of learning workers should be provided opportunities to help them uncover new fields in which to overcome and advance. This emphasis requires a new and diverse management philosophy, which would introduce new methods, tools and practices, focusing on the workgroups and utilizing their competencies to focus on efficiency and effectiveness within the company. MUSCO, an Iowa lighting company looked into introducing Shakespearean studies in training classes such as Electrical Wiring. The company's management believes connecting the two disciplines will bring their worlds closer and create an ideal employee. Augmenting one's education adds strengths, and broadens a person's self-confidence in their ability to perform. The feeling is that it is better to be one % better at a thousand things than one thousand % better at one thing. Through this focus an employee will develop greater confidence, increased enjoyment at work and a superior ability to achieve desired outcomes. Hewlett-Packard's ex-CEO Carly Fiorina stated in her commencement address at Stanford University that her studying the shift of the Middle Ages to the Renaissance helped her in understanding the digital age progression.

Before human capital measurements are possible, organizations need to determine the correlation linking the training and business outcomes desired. Upon determining the correlation they must implement an assessment process that will determine a *Return on Investment* (ROI) from additional employee training and development. Since humans are the most effective intellectual force, this process mandates equipping management with a new generation of techniques, tools and methods in hopes of providing support to identifying and managing the organization's investment in its collective knowledge warehouse. It is critical therefore, that these processes are designed with decided ideas in mind.

The business decisions managers make daily have to be weighed against the business benefits sought. Managers must appraise whether the resources committed directly or indirectly by their assessment are likely to meet strategic objectives. The composite effect of these results will eventually affect both the undertaking and the satisfying of the strategic initiatives, making it essential that the workers are involved with and assessed in a proactive manner. When the organization's competencies assessed are determined to be intangible, placing a price on them is complicated, yet basic if its human assets are to allow it to increase its book value.

Placing a value on an intangible introduces a variety of concerns. First, the organization is faced with the ethical issue of how to keep investors aware of the company's worth. Second, management needs to determine how to improve their understanding of their worker's human capital and finally if intangibles are to be measured, they should know how to use them. In some situations, companies are valued above book value, and as studies indicate the ratio of book to market value for Dow Jones Industrial companies is about half that of knowledge-intense companies such as Microsoft. This premium overbook value is representative of the people, its technological advances and product releases on top of its future expected offerings.

The belief that a company is solely value-based on tangibles such as buildings and machinery is changing. Today only 6 to 30% of a company's worth is obtained from tangible assets. The service industry no longer has a need for huge buildings in order to do its work; the critical wealth is now people with ideas, and they can be located anywhere. Microsoft is an example of a company whose assets are the imaginations of its employees who generate nothing tangible and that has developed a reputation for products thought to be superior for personal computer users. Other companies, those generating Microsoft's products, execute the production of its ideas. As a company, Microsoft has placed strategies in place to drive growth and is recognized for its human capital, which gives it new, additional capabilities and greater worth.

Established accounting still lacks competent methods for assigning value to the intangible assets a company will use for future planning. Measuring human capital has not proven to be a straightforward process, but companies are gradually finding methods to do so. Skandia AFS, a Swedish corporation, uses an *Intellectual Capital Annual Report* using its "Navigator" process model to measure its human capital. The one hundred or so measurements developed and designated in the report gauge Skandia's internal and external forces to judge their effect on the company. Since Skandia was the forerunner of these measurements, it had no benchmark to use, but the company developed ratios measuring elements that help in shaping its success or failure. The characteristic measurements developed range from employee turnover, indicating organizational stability, to sales per customer, which determines efficiency to its customers. By applying these measurements management is able to determine how effectively employees are used and how efficient they are in addressing customer issues.

Management attempting to identify the benefits employees bring to an organization typically uses the following measurement:

$$\textit{Profits per employee} = \frac{\textit{Corporation Profits}}{\textit{Number of employees}}$$

$$\textit{Output per employee} = \frac{\textit{Units produced or processed}}{\textit{Number of employees}}$$

In each of these, the efficiency of the employees validates how well the organization is using its human capital in performing what it focuses on, whereas measuring its effectiveness validates how well an organization has directed attention to its end results. Either measurement will illustrate the productivity by the organization, making more products by means of the same number or by decreasing the number of employees and maintaining the same production levels. The objective of measuring human capital should be to determine how well the organization is performing, how it compares to the competition, and whether or not it is improving in essence how can it be used to make the company more effective, profitable and competitive. It is my belief that with the corporate world's growing interest in the importance of human capital we can expect to see accountants and financial analysts using assorted measurements for these intangible assets in the future.

Thompson and Strickland[5] (1990) defined corporate culture as "the way we do things around here." Given that culture affects everybody in the company, it follows a human capital environment involves everyone from the CEO down to the person at the lowest level of the corporate structure. Given an opportunity, each member will provide human capital to his or her own domain of influence. For complete success, it is essential that the entire organization be bound by values underlying its vision and mission that speak to human capital. This requires a long-term allegiance, where management forms and employs a strategic leadership style.

Educational System Problems

No two identical intellect levels exist, nor do the sundry levels have the same importance. Many recruits entering the workplace for the first time often suffer from a deficiency of essential skills and competencies, whereas many of those, the mature workers have, are out-dated. Regardless of which, workers require rudimentary skills to function in everyday situations, but for effective use of added knowledge, education is the obligatory key element, presenting a major challenge to train and develop people in today's dynamic business state.

With intelligence becoming the new center of property and wealth, companies are dependent on an educational system incapable of providing a continual source of qualified knowledge workers. The United States literacy rate has dropped to a level where it is no longer in the top 50 countries. There have been several studies that found many graduates from universities such as Brown, Harvard, Vanderbilt, and Carnegie Mellon lacking in the compulsory critical thinking and communication skills required for today's workplace. Too many students leaving high school are not prepared for higher education work. In many cases their reading, writing and math skills are still at the elementary level. These findings concurred with an article by the American Management Association (AMA)[6] that reported at least one-third (34%) of job applicants lacked the needed skills to perform the jobs sought. Using the most recent data from the U.S. Department of Education the percentage of students who graduate from high school was estimated to be 70% of those who enter high school and only 32% of all students graduating are qualified to attend a four-year institution of higher learning. It appears High School students are now taking five to six years to earn their diplomas similar to University and College graduates. All indications are that recent graduation percentages are dropping in intellect levels to such an extent that American corporations are losing the battle for recruits capable of functioning in the new workplace.

In 1992, United States Secretary of Labor Lynn Martin formed the "*The Secretary's Commission on Achieving Necessary Skills (SCANS)* [7]." The Commission was to determine and study the several competencies and skills believed critical for an individual to be successful in the 21st century workplace. This movement was a take-off of a program ("*A Nation at Risk"),* introduced in 1982 by President Reagan. The outcome of this study, *"SCANS Report for America 2000",* identified five essential competencies; (1) assigning resources in the course of their work, (2) *Interpersonal* skills possessed by individuals allowing them to function in teams, whether serving or leading, and being able to negotiate and perform the work themselves, (3) *Information* that could be used in the attainment, evaluation, organization, maintenance, analysis, communication and understanding of the processes involved, (4) *Systems* allowing one to understand complex relationships, which could be monitored, corrected, improved and designed, (5) *Technology* by which individuals are capable of making a variety of selections and are able to align, maintain and trouble-shoot. In addition to the above mentioned skills the following were included; *Cognitive and Thinking/Social Skills and Personal Qualities.*

At the outset, introduced as a five-year plan[8] entitled "*Learning a Living: A Blueprint for High Performance,"* the SCAN 2000 program aka AM2000 was meant to define the expertise needed in the workplace. In spite of what Washington and local school systems may claim, the findings suggest a failure since the proposed plan was intended to use established schools to train students in the trades rather than in knowledge type work. Although American companies were moving from a manufacturing to information-intensive service setting, Washington was proposing vocational training for students contrary to the needs of the economy. The premise behind the effort was an excellent one, but unless there is a complete mobilization of the country's resources an effort such as this will never thrive. I cannot help but remember reading the reasons civilizations fall is that the compulsory steps are not taken far enough in advance to prevent a crisis, and that the mandatory training and education is of greater sophistication than proposed. Hayek[10] stated that ". . . our present society lacks such conscious direction toward a single aim, that its activities are guided by the whims and fancies of irresponsible individuals . . ."

In much the same manner that Charles Handy[9] came to the realization of the Sigmoid Curve one can easily identify their standing. Personally, I have come to understand how the curve plays a major role in any learning. Regardless of what an individual or organization undertakes, the starting point is always followed with some experimentation from which one may falter for a time, and then move to rapid improvements in performance, productivity, growth and ultimately substantial gain. The progression however, does not continue forever, and at a point the process begins to slow down, plateau and wane. I couldn't help thinking about the stock market recently and what has transpired.

In his book, Handy states that " . . . *by the time you know where you ought to go, it's too late to go there, or more dramatically, if you keep on going the way you are, you will miss the road to the future*." He explains how the curve provides an understanding of the ups and downs of life for both the personnel and organizations as in Figure 8. Handy argues the need for workers and/or companies to transform starting at *Point A* while they are successful and not when they reach the point of decline at *Point B*. Figure 8 details a compelling image of how companies transform, and when the level of decline is reached they discover it is often too late to recover. The process to reduce the disparity between points A and B requires about six to eighteen months. Often companies operate under the *Icarus Paradox*[10] when processes that may have worked well previously are attempted, may no longer be effective.

Individual's Work Life – Sigmoid Curve

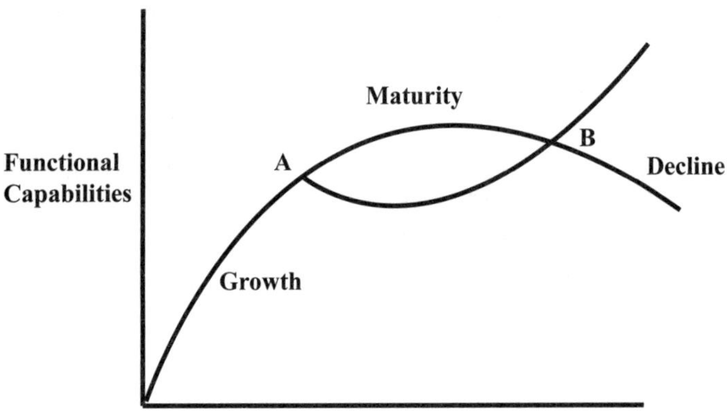

Figure 8

The ideal situation is having the capability to anticipate and identify at what spot the next wave will occur in order to continue the upward progression before the current one recedes. Yet what often occurs is an effort to alter direction at *Point B* when disaster is possibly knocking at the door. Handy's theory may stem from Thom's Catastrophe Theory[11], a mathematical model explaining why sharply discontinuous events often occur. Thom's theory fell out of favor seeing as it was unable to predict when the alteration would take place. I often wonder, if we were to apply this theory to the need for education in the U.S., have we possibly passed point B, making it too late to implement corrective and even preventative actions?

The conclusions from every commission formed to study the problem of school competencies state the American educational system has reached a level of mediocrity, which cannot help but affect our future as a society. American students are learning less when compared to their parents or students in other countries, especially at a time when our best learning systems are only capable of delivering a fraction of the knowledge workers require to perform their jobs effectively. I have attempted for years to refrain from becoming emotionally overwrought at the mistakes and misdeeds of Washington's agencies responsible for our educational systems. Still, it is difficult not to be saddened, realizing that although our governing leaders discuss education, disagreeing with the numbers, they have an inability to unearth the right solution to prepare our youth for the 21st century economy. There seems to be no concern to justify what they are doing. Rather than reviewing the industrial methods, institutional organizations, pedagogy and curriculum used to improve the educational system little appears to be done to improve the system, and in fact education is still the first area cut when costs are addressed. This is truly unfortunate since the truth about such a problematic topic appears to be ignored by those who don't want to be inconvenienced. In fact, education did not appear to be one of the top five major concerns emphasized by the recent governmental candidates at all levels.

If the educational systems are determined to develop a labor force that operates similar to robots, doing as told, and never questioning, they are succeeding. On the other hand, if our educational systems are striving to prepare our students to integrate into a world-class workforce similar to what Japan, Taiwan, Germany, France, India, Ireland and other countries have, we are failing. Students should be prepared to direct their efforts to rapid adjustment as they enter into an information age of global production. Admittedly, the

American educational system does require improvement and needs to be addressed differently if it is to have an impact on performance and productivity. Unfortunately, the American population has fallen in line and continues to accept these errors in judgment, unwilling to take preventive measures in advance of a crisis. Unwilling to face reality, Americans cling to the faith their children will receive the education essential to thrive, without realizing the demand for educated workers is growing more rapidly than our educational system can provide. We have an obligation to be open-minded enough to acknowledge the growing education problem before it is too late, and address the problems, challenges, and issues of developing a labor force capable of addressing the 21st Century economy.

Sharing To Improve Knowledge

Few workers have correct or sufficient knowledge to solve the increasingly complex problems confronting them, validating the necessity for the sharing of knowledge resources. Once deemed to be a major barrier, distance has ceased to be an obstacle to accessing and sharing human capital. A more critical problem is the lack of time available for workers to expand their learning even by way of the new technology. A still bigger obstacle might be management's control or lack of, preventing access to the vast amounts of knowledge and information obtainable, such as through the Internet. Although individuals may learn and further enhance their responsibilities by accessing the Internet, many companies prohibit or discourage web surfing. In 2003, Websense an internet research group determined that Corporations lose as much as $85 Billion a year in lost productivity when employees freely access the internet. Yet, while workers devote approximately 25% of their work time in search of information, which 50% of what they find is of no use, they are prohibited from using this valuable resource where 60% of the required information is located. Google is accessed with over 2.5 Billion inquiries a month, causing one to wonder who answered these questions before this search tool became available, and it is only one of many browsers one can use for assistance. This is an interesting obstacle, because while workers are permitted to play games such as solitaire on their PCs in hopes of relieving stress and frustration, researching for information, which might help them in their work, is prohibited. If companies were to permit access to this phenomenal amount of information via web technologies personnel would be provided increased information, enhanced collaboration and the capability to use it more effectively. Through the drive for continual learning and the strength of the Internet in harnessing knowledge, limiting access to this resource reduces an organization's dominance, innovation, creativity, and growth.

For a company to be able to leapfrog competitive challenges it is vital that its personnel are focused to participating and introducing dramatic new ideas, not only by way of the internal workforce, but also through the workers accessing the internet in a value-added method, recognized as mass collaboration. The emergence of new low-cost collaborative infrastructures such as MySpace, YouTube, Linus and Wikipedia has increased the availability of local and globally based intelligence due to social networking. If organizations are to utilize their workforce's awareness they must be persistent in keeping them focused and permitting the practical application of their knowledge supported by common sense. To do so, it is critical that the workers are able to utilize the knowledge accessible quickly and be able to share areas of expertise and expand further from the feedback received.

Progress is impossible without change, and those who cannot change their minds cannot change anything.
George Bernard Shaw

Chapter 5

An Industry Evolution – An Obsession to Succeed

Throughout history, companies have always responded to scarce resources, and now at a time when relevant human capital is determined to be a key strategic weapon, small islands of directed efforts are becoming evident. Little appears to have been learned of the methods transformed in leveraging and managing human capital in the last decade. Although companies know their human capital should be utilized differently, they continue to use them solely in efforts to survive. They never seem to have sufficient time or resources to devote to defining and designing at the beginning of a project, and then suffer later when things have to be band-aided in hopes of stopping the bleeding since things aren't progressing properly. Although the importance of human capital is realized, organizations are destroying the social systems that generate the asset essential for the millennia, exhausting it as it exits out the door by way of the continued mergers, re-engineering efforts, plant closures and a declining knowledgeable labor force. As the social systems are destroyed, employees lose any loyalty that may come with permanent employment. Any motivation and interest for exerting extra effort and customer-focus for quality service disappears. One such example is the outcome of the merger stuck between America West and US Airways. Almost three years after the merger employees still think of themselves as members of two separate airlines, and believe the company will split shortly, reverting back to separate airlines. Those who were not let go lost seniority and salary, and are bitter and often rude and arrogant to customers.

The agility, innovation, creativity, responsibility, and technology required to compete in the 21st Century requires an open, collaborative atmosphere led by a system coinciding with a shift in business processes, methods and protocol fostering a knowledge environment. Management needs to be a guiding light, working close to those who choose to contribute and work to motivate those who do not share their human capital. To arrive at the advantage desired one should to have a strategic vision to direct the company in developing and maintaining an atmosphere that fosters and rewards the sharing and utilization of human capital. As such, it is a requirement that human capital be rooted in the organization's vision as it is a consequence of strategy. If there is little positive effect from this strategic process, the effort will prove to be meaningless and the company will strive in its attempt to gain an advantage.

Improvement Will Require Change

The year 2000 brought a new century and the first generation of a new millennium, some even referred to it as the end to an old civilization. With business moving from competitive shifts in price to improved quality and speed, the latter part of the 20th Century brought profound and rapid conversion. These alterations are forcing companies to make effective use of their human capital.

In this hyper-turbulent atmosphere companies must continually renew themselves to survive. They must know when adjustment is required and should be able to translate their energy and ability to meet and implement needed revision. About 80% of all new jobs created in the last decade have been in the service industry, yet management is still employing methods applied in the industrial era to address the issues brought into play in this new work environment. Since today's practices may no longer be applicable to future problems, focusing on the human capital available is crucial. Einstein[2] indicated the need for a different thought process when he wrote, "The significant problems we face cannot be solved at the same level of thinking we were at when we created them."

Change in Management Responsibilities

Change is critical in today's corporate environment and workers need to be prepared to anticipate, drive, support, or respond in order to take action. The infrastructure essential to support a knowledge-enabled system is not like any other because the method used is distinctive. Therefore, management cannot address human capital in the same manner as physical assets unless it is through a human centered process. This technique will allow a business to tap into its workforce's intellect and uncover individual assets that will assist them in recognizing and valuing prior learning. Such a powerful line of attack can be explosive, but it has to be reconfigured in ways to elicit, collect, develop and transfer knowledge to influence information. Consequently, the modification detected by design and decision-making will be simplified.

Management must understand the benefits of capturing and sharing learning, as they often fail to understand how to put thc process into action. The trained expert may know best how to recognize or extract information, but in some cases, the gorilla or brute force method to elicit information is perhaps more advantageous and rewarding. Current decisions are often made to address problems that may have been challenging earlier, but given that information involving earlier conclusions was never recorded, is lost or cannot be recalled, incorrect verdicts are made, often leading to failure. These situations can be attributed to two possibilities; first, the decision-maker lacks sufficient information to make a correct decision; and secondly, large amounts of information are coming from all directions, and it is becoming more complex to determine what is and is not important. In either situation some information and methods for conducting business are no longer valid and a manager or employee who refuses to continue learning for whatever reason to replenish this obsolescence is soon left behind. Another problem area confronting management is their focusing on short-term outcomes. Although this direction may lead a company to meet its objectives for a period, unless other aspects of performance are accounted for, it will fail. Studies imply that a major contributor to the competitive loss by American corporations is due to their myopia (short-sightedness). For example, in the early 1960's, RCA and Westinghouse were involved in introducing the AM-LCD (Liquid Crystal Display) technology used today in laptop and notebook personal computers, in addition to many other common critical components. Neither company however, would commit to long-term funding and eventually lost the market to corporations that did, NEC, Toshiba and Sharp. A study by deGeus[3] while with the Royal Shell Company revealed one third of the companies listed on the Fortune 500 in 1970 had disappeared by 1983. Some had survived for seventy-five years or longer, but for every one that survived two eventually failed. Pan American, Penn Central Railroad, RCA, Wang, Smith Corona, and DEC are corporations that failed due to their inability to recreate themselves sooner than their competitors. These enterprises were ignorant of new ventures and opportunities that might allow them to grow, and today many are no different as failures continue. Failing companies have warning signs, but their blinders prevent them from realizing what is occurring. Size has nothing to do with success as 200 or more Fortune 500 companies continued to disappear in the 1980s, 90s and now the 2000s. This trend continues today with the demise of some once dominant in the United States, such as Westinghouse, Montgomery Ward, COMPAQ, Arthur Anderson, and Allied Signal. Recently, we witnessed the trend continuing with the failures of Lehman Brothers, Bear Stearns, Wachovia and Washington Mutual Banks, and it is anticipated others will follow.

Group or Individual Transformation

The transition to the information age is challenged by the problem of the growing lack of competent and skilled workers in many industries. This shortage requires that Human Resource (HR) management take a proactive role in an organization's development stressing the people-related components of continuity planning, life-long learning and collaboration rather than only individual learning. A new requirement of Human Resource managers is to help determine who is core to the business system, and what skills and competencies are necessary to create a labor force that is highly creative and strategic to the organization's competitive quest.

Before the Information Age, an individual's personality traits, natural inclinations and particular aptitude were determined by output directed toward a common good. Skills were passed from one generation to another through apprentice programs where an individual would work among Master craftsmen until all aspects of a particular trade had been mastered. Later, the apprentice would be replaced by semi-skilled workers who would perform fewer and easier tasks in their particular job. Now in the Information Age, technology has altered the methods workers use to perform their work and the manner by which they communicate. The new developments in technology have helped in introducing new methods for effective storage and the accessing of human capital. At the same time, these technological developments have generated additional stress because people have become so reliant on technological equipment such as PC's and cell phones to do their work and communicate (e-mail) they become stressed, anxious and irritable when a problem is experienced.

Getting People Involved

Workers function more effectively if their work surroundings are pleasing. In a gratifying setting the workforce learns more rapidly, enhances their relationships with others, creates and delivers more effective results, and takes greater risks. Many people once considered critical to the organization are seldom given sufficient training to do other work and are let go when their jobs are eliminated. When given little or no training and development they feel rejected or ignored, often leave their creativity at home and are unwilling to contribute. Employees, who are unhappy or receive little or no satisfaction from the workplace, are reluctant to go to work, often calling in with a false illness, if a call is even made. Believing they are on a one-way street with no benefits, under utilized workers are often categorized as non-value added commodities and ultimately placed into matrix quadrants that designate a lack of sufficient or correct intellect. These employees are actually abused when managers fail to understand or develop them.

Companies are often the least responsive to change. Once it establishes a successful technology or process, a company may have difficulty discarding it in favor of a newer one which may work better and even cost less. Wang lost its dominance in office technology when it failed to address the surge in demand for the desktop PC in the office. Compaq grew to be the number one supplier for business, but failed to maintain its initiative when the company chose to ignore the PC home usage. IBM's share of the mainframe computer market was once nearly 80%, but the company almost went out of business when it hesitated to move into the PC market. The have since moved out of this market and are concentrating on the service industry. Xerox lost a large amount of its copier market-share position when it failed to renew its patents while some companies, have realized that what may have worked historically may not work in the future. Radio Shack for one remains a viable company given that it determined it could not compete successfully in the PC market, and changed its focus to the component, entertainment and technological areas supporting this market. In the 21st century, companies face new challenges, problems and possibilities, all demanding new creative solutions and strategies, which require flexible, innovative and creative people to face them.

Although the knowledge emphasis has not been noticeably identified, all learning results in adjustment, even that as an outcome of failures and setbacks. A 21st century organization should be concerned with the dissimilar areas involved. All areas altered are inter-related and when one is affected, the future behavior, attitudes, intellect of others or both can be altered. Conversion comes as a consequence of workers being motivated and willing to learn how to do things in an unlike and better method. When people learn and develop new competencies what they do and understand is modified. By way of adjustment, they develop a different insight of the world around them and therefore organizations change. The root of all transformation is attitude, which stimulates potential, influences behaviors and ultimately performance. If an individual has a negative, uninviting attitude, little constructive modification will occur, but those with a proactive attitude believe the possibilities are unlimited.

Developing intelligence requires acceptable execution and determined effort. People have a duty to learn and be committed to doing something about it. If an individual were to study a particular subject for one hour a day, everyday, s/he would be an expert in the particular subject at the end of a year. Not too difficult, yet so fulfilling. I recall meeting Frank McIntosh, the inventor of high quality stereo systems. In his seventies when I first met him, he told me he spent two hours each day learning something new. He was studying surveying when I first met him, and even though he was too old to be licensed, he was studying to fly a helicopter when I last saw him. Like McIntosh, Peter Drucker[4] mastered a new subject every three or four years to where he offered his new learning by offering college courses in the subject matter. Forbes magazine once described him as having the youngest mind.

Intellect gained by means of the senses is commonly regarded as compelling and longer lasting than that developed from abstract methods such as reading. Goethe[5] spent an hour each morning in his garden studying the elements, and his intuitive awareness sharpened to where he was able to accurately predict the weather. In later years when he no longer worked in his garden he found he had lost his forecasting ability. Knowledge is not an end in itself however, what a company does by means of its human capital determines its worth. At one time, it may have been important to know someone, but in today's setting it comes down to what a person knows and how their human capital can be used.

By means of the technological capabilities existing today, globalization places all enterprises on an equal level. Thomas Friedman[6] wrote "*As globalization gives everyone the same information, resources, technology and markets, a society's or organization's particular ability to put these pieces together in the fastest and most innovative manner separates the winners and the losers in the global economy.*" Those relying on technology and its capabilities soon recognize other enterprises have the same advantage, as a genuinely global company has no physical or regional limitations.

As companies move from the *Industrial* to the *Information Age,* they face demanding challenges requiring strong globalization strategies. Any wanting to expand throughout the globe often lack the resources or capability on how to identify indispensable global competencies, leverage and replicate best practices, and employ their human capital in a meaningful manner. These challenges are reflected in today's workplace, family life and individual morality. Directing efforts toward meeting these challenges brings economic growth to individual and organizational potential, over and above creativity and innovation.

Regardless of where workers are globally located, if given the technology, access to the same resources and the capability to share awareness learning is indeed possible. This sharing is the might of knowledge; its use by one person does not inhibit its use by others. Unless workers have the flexibility, technical excellence, agility, drive, resilience, comprehension and development opportunities, they will be unable to address emergent problems. It has been proven that an investment in first-rate human capital practices will help in producing bottom-line benefits and minimize employee mobility. Enterprises that develop their personnel on an on-going process, creating opportunities for them to collect, synthesize and manage understanding, will realize greater efficiency and profits. Ironically, in many situations when people are let go from the workplace due to a lack of skills and competencies they often become the entrepreneurs who successfully introduce new ventures. Some even come into direct competition with their previous employers.

Ackoff[7] believes what workers know is far less important than what can be done with their knowledge. In American business, creativity and innovation are often attributed to youth. In contrast, Asian countries as a rule equate wisdom with age, so youth is often a deterrent for a senior management position. Since learning drives the innovation process, Asians believe those possessing added knowledge and competencies that usually comes with age are best suited to lead. In the West, however, managers seems to disregard wisdom and competency, limiting the use of human capital for the benefit of the organization.

To experience a sense of achievement, employees need to know that they are gaining familiarity, becoming more innovative and efficient and functioning in a challenging situation. Creating significant roles and responsibilities helps workers develop a sense of ownership and loyalty resulting in greater contributions to the organization. As individuals become adept in their assigned tasks, they can be given additional responsibilities with added difficulty. Workers want to learn what is needed and when they are unable to gain knowledge due to the lack of time, training and resources not being offered, they often develop low self-esteem, and ultimately negatively affect the organization.

New Competencies Required

Current methods reshaping the manner work can be satisfied is through the use of new knowledge. Knowledge doubled between 1750 and 1900, expanding ten-fold in the first half of the 20th century and a thousand times more since then, yet even with their human capital, many workers still lack an understanding of how to truly perform their jobs. Workers remain the critical aspect of the process and those possessing the appropriate skills and competencies are of greater substance than those who do not. Unfortunately, 80% of today's workforce lacks these requirements in addition to experience working on teams, and problem solving abilities to be truly effective in the workplace. By referencing Debra Amidon's Kaleidoscope theory[8], it is possible to visualize the similarity of the many technological possibilities. If workers had the crucial human capital the varied conclusions would be intensified, as with each turn of a kaleidoscope. An element giving meaning to the diverse aspects of data and information and putting it into a useable form to be used for an enhanced understanding is required. As such, it becomes necessary to reflect on the telecommunications revolution coming into the global environment. An understanding of cellular, satellite transmission, fiber optics and wireless communications are just the beginning of the new waves of technology in which many of today's workers lack the essential skills.

Transformation

Transformation is like a dam; once it breaks loose it is impossible to stop. A gradual process that entails the breaking of old habits and creating new ones has to be managed with compassion and understanding, with a full range of options for the resisters. As with all organizational conversion efforts resistance is natural. People do not like change; they find it frightening, but do not resist for long changes that benefit them to the extent as those that threaten them. When change is debated, many refer to the process as transformation rather than change, yet the Greek word *Metanoia* might be better used in its place. Where transformation implies variation in form, shape or appearance, Metanoia implies penitence, repentance and reorientation of one's attitude to life and spiritual conversion. This holistic makeover is where employee training and development should be directed. With deficiencies in competencies, talent and ability require attention, making a new focus supported by innovative thinking vital. Therefore, change requires an open, flexible eco-system among those who are able to think and act with speed, agility and focus. The rational of changing an organization's customs is often the effect of a troubled situation as those continually going through a modification process may often miss developments and the needs in their environment. The current corporate focus should center on the people, knowledge, expertise and processes involved. Therefore, in addition to these, it is the employee's skills, competencies and capacity to adjust in companies that are flexible, fast or aggressive that determines transformation in achieving an unprecedented competitive force.

There are two reasons for developing a transformation strategy: (1) a leader determining a need for developing a new focus, and (2) the economic situation forcing modification, bringing the awareness and fundamental objective to serve customers and win over the competition. Although it is easier for organizations to transform when in a crisis state, change undertaken in non-crisis situations usually fails, often leaving them in a mediocre situation. For change to go well it is essential to know *Why* it is needed, clarifying all *Why Now* reasons, which detail benefits from success or penalties from failure. To do so, will require that all workers understand *where* the transformation is to take the organization, and simplify for all involved, *What's* in it for them, should they participate?

In deciding to infuse a business scheme, one of the first things an organization does is locate someone who is knowledgeable in the methodology. This effort is followed with numerous activities; introductory plans, meetings, discussions, presentations of line of attack, reports, financials and the sharing of assorted information, thoughts and ideas. Throughout it all workers become psyched up and excited about starting the process. Yet later, if someone were to ask those involved how the deployment was progressing, a variety of excuses might be heard; too many things happening, problems surfacing in areas not expected, and not enough time or resources. Again, still later, if the same queries were asked, additional excuses would be heard; End-of-Month/End-of-Quarter problems, demands for products and services, etc. In both situations there would be words of encouragement and continued hope that the transformation would begin.

What makes the management of these organizations typical? These are individuals properly motivated, who know what they want, but somehow cannot bring themselves to getting the jobs or projects started. Over and over, efforts such as those described are repeated in business. It is as though there is an unstated belief that once a decision to implement a business tactic is made, nothing else is required. Other than attending meetings, listening to or giving presentations and reporting, management feels there is little else required on their part and consequently, little is accomplished. Unfortunately, what is described is management. Exceptional, talented individuals who are afraid to make a mistake and unable to make a decision and execute it. These managers spend a large amount of time in meetings and never really get to understand the company's needs and how they can improve their operations. What needs to be done is to recognize and reward those who take risks and even make mistakes, but because of fear they spend upwards of 45% of their time making choices founded on intuition and gut feelings rather than with facts and data. Basing decisions in this manner will statistically result in inaccurate judgments 70% of the time, whereas flipping a coin will result in incorrect decisions only 50% of the time.

In studying leaders one can visualize Jack Welch, ex CEO of GE who was adamant with GE's introduction of six-sigma to its workforce. Welch studied the methodology thoroughly and was proactive in determining its potential and the requirements needed for success before he deployed the system to the corporation. He determined that to be successful a conversion in culture was vital; personnel at all levels in the different GE businesses would have to buy into the methodology, be committed and involved, beginning with himself. He had HR put a process into effect that no one would get a promotion or a salary increase until they became Six Sigma certified. To demonstrate his buy-in he became Green Belt certified and completed cost reduction projects. In contrast, many leaders of other corporations did not exhibit commitment and being involved, and as a consequence their implementation of six-sigma ultimately failed. There was never a total responsibility to having all personnel involved, least of all management, who attempted to implement the methodology piece-meal. The outcome has been GE recognizing cost savings in the billions, progressing beyond addressing the low-hanging fruit and sharing cost savings with their customers. It is unfortunate, but many companies that have attempted to implement the philosophy have had minimal effects in comparison and some have ultimately dropped the effort after spending hundreds of millions of dollars. I believe the reason for this failure is due to the lack of trust, which leads to the lack of commitment and ultimately failure. It should be noted that the results are similar to implementing any methodology such as MBO, TQM and Re-engineering.

Leaders are difficult to unearth. One example of an illustrious leader was Sam Walton.[9] The founder of Wal-Mart visited all of his stores unannounced at least once a year to interact with the store associates. He paid attention to how things were done, listened and accumulated information so he might determine what and how their work might be made easier. Mr. Walton knew that to listen, to truly listen, meant paying attention to what was being said beneath the words. Through this method he created an informal and formless network that made him aware of ways the operations of his stores could be improved. Walton believed, in theory, that since the associates he spoke with were performing the particular operations, they would have an understanding of how to improve them, and all he had to do was listen to them and then act to make the feasible changes. By applying this unconventional manner he was able to determine how the workers were treated. He believed if he was compassionate, just, fair, and caring to his employees they would treat customers in the same manner. Fortunately, Walton is not the only leader who values his employees. Conglomerates such as Wegman's supermarket chain (rated the best U.S. company to work for by Fortune Magazine), Starbucks, FedEx, Pella Windows, Medtronics, and of course Southwest Airlines, are all led by managers who recognize the importance of his employees.

Ultimately, the end result may be a question of belief. It often appears people just do not seem to believe in themselves. We must not look down at the decision makers who give the appearance of behaving in an unfavorable manner when trying to implement something desired with all their heart, and end up failing. Periodically, things desired are somehow sabotaged by the method used to achieve them. These are the focal yet selective details that do not help in reaching personal objectives, but contribute to a lost direction. Often, people dream about a future worth having, a place where dreams come true, a life with meaning and one in which a contribution to the world can be made, leaving it a little better. Too often however, those working for what they want are too concerned about the small details of life, and may lack the understanding of how to reach the situation where dreams come true. Then for some reason these same people quit dreaming and become what I refer to as, if people; *if only I had done this or if only I had done that.* They are the ones who recap their life story and wish they had done something they hadn't. Utilizing human capital effectively may be the answer people are looking for and the direction needed to get there. The only requirement is buy-in and a strong belief in oneself.

Higher values are placed on companies that improve their bottom-line by way of natural growth rather than cost cutting efforts such as employee reductions. Retaining the right personnel provides a source of advantage not easily duplicated and if management has the ability to manage these workers effectively they have a competitive edge that can be sustained and even strengthened. It is becoming apparent American companies have suffered significant talent losses amounting to a high cost. Especially where trying to find and retain high-quality people. Gary Reiner, as GE's Chief Information Officer estimated an approximate cost of $100,000 to find a high-quality information management professional and cost upwards of another $150,000 and up to a year for this individual to be fully productive. Squandering workers is estimated to cost billions of dollars each year in lost productivity and human capital, substantiating the importance of keeping employee turnover to a minimum. One might wonder if the reason productivity in the American economy has not grown quicker is a consequence of the many workforce layoffs experienced. Repeatedly, the reason for an organization's inability to thrive is management forgetting its personnel are the key to performance and ultimately productivity.

Relationships are Systems

A *system* is made up of all of the combined processes, functions and tasks essential to accomplishing a given or stated aim. In a systems setting, organizations can be thought of as complex living processes working in balance with one another and interacting dynamically with a supposed common purpose and identity. In social networking systems thinking a concern for and attention paid to relationships are essential. They are the forces that affect interactions allowing for appropriate behavior, values, norms, beliefs and synergism to develop networking. Systems require surroundings where workers are allowed to develop in-depth associations among peers, suppliers and customers. Relationships in conjunction with a moral foundation of honesty, trust, respect and reciprocity often take years to develop and come about from the special status one holds with regards to others.

Only accompanied by these traits is it possible to facilitate human capital and identify what is known; who has it, and an understanding of how it can be used in conjunction with what we do not know that we should. In a people focused system there ought to be a concern for and attention paid to relationships. It is by means of a network of relationships among those who have an understanding of the organization and its subsystems that information and knowledge travel. Relationships connecting workers across an organization is what shapes its culture and something that cannot be written into a conventional job description. It is through an individual's ability to learn, collaborate, and innovate faster, that gives an organization a sustainable source of competitive advantage. Humans require relationships to function properly and emotional support and reverence from others to form an upright relationship affecting proper connections, which allows development of the synergy required to harness collective human capital.

Overwhelming the Organization with Knowledge

It is essential that 21st century organizations develop an original frame of mind. The diverse mindsets must be contrasted to assess the limitations of the old contemplating with what a new *out of the box* mindset would include. It is critical that we transform from the hierarchical system Frederick Taylor[12], the father of *Scientific Management* believed, as detailed in the following quote:

> *Hardly a competent workman can be found who does not devote a considerable amount of time to studying just how slowly he can work and still convince his employer that he is going at a good*

> *pace. Under our system a worker is told just what he is to do and how he is to do it. Any improvement he makes upon the orders given to him is fatal to his success.*

It was Taylor's belief; systems should be set up to prevent workers from using their minds. Under his system, only the managers should be allowed to use their minds and the worker is not to think. Workers are to come to work in body only. Thinking is the responsibility and purpose of management, who supposedly possess superior intelligence and specialized awareness. Taylor believed the workers would achieve higher production if management's orders and direction were followed.

In contrast, the beliefs of Knonsuke Matsushita[13], the founder and head of Matsushita Electric, Ltd are just the opposite. His quote given at an American Business Leaders Conference indicates the difference.

> *We are going to win and the industrial west is going to lose out, there's not much you can do about it because the reasons for your failure are within yourselves. With your bosses doing the thinking while the workers wield the screwdrivers, you're convinced deep down that this is the right way to run a business. For you the essence of management is getting the ideas out of the heads of the bosses and into the hands of labor.*

What Mr. Matsushita is saying is unless workers are allowed to be themselves and contribute, the company will fail. To a large extent, in today's environment management evaluates and ranks their workers, creating a competitive atmosphere connecting those who are trying to impress management. As a rule, corporations direct large sums of money toward their recruiting process, hiring supposedly qualified, educated individuals to fill established, varying sets of roles. New recruits are brought into a setting that might be compared to a game of golf, with its barriers and obstacles. New recruits are provided the best set of golf clubs (computers, software, tools, etc.) then assigned an objective of achieving 18 holes in 18 strokes. The golf course traps and bunkers (organizational silos, lack of training, bureaucracy, archaic policies and procedures) are some examples of the obstacles confronting new resources. Management gives the impression it still believes in and relies on the same set of skills it has used for years. By providing personnel with bigger golf clubs or long distance balls (desktop computers and additional software), managers believe employees will be able to solve all problems confronted. Unfortunately, organizations often forget that their decisive objectives are to improve functioning and strengthen competitiveness, something possible by managing their talent.

The best performers (the long ball hitters with the better scores) are usually those who may have greater understanding, a more profound network of relationships or are provided opportunities to excel. Beyond this, management does little to enhance the employee's development. Instead of promoting a system of collaboration, where the employees team up functioning as a community to determine how they might alter the course, making it easier for all of them to get a hole in one, management simply labels the remaining employees as *poor performers.* Forcing them to compete against each other makes it difficult for individuals to work in concert, often resulting in a loss of valuable resources. Functioning as a community, working to remove the obstacles in their way workers perform better problem-solving and can in due course triumph in mastering the 18 holes in 18 strokes. This is where rewarding instead of penalizing errors and mistakes comes into play and learning is suppressed. The one question presented whenever something wrong occurs should be altered from *Who* did it, to *Why* did this happen?

The atmosphere has unfortunately, become one where workers are protective of their knowledge and believe their importance and advancement is contingent on their demonstrating unique and exceptional intellect. In essence, an environment where *"Managers are the ones who manage and the workers are the ones who work"* will ultimately lead to the destruction of the system.

What is required for greater success is communicating the sharing of knowledge, ideas and expertise in a collaborative environment where management runs interference by breaking down barriers and removing obstacles. Communications is central to the multitude of competencies involved in an organization's human capital seeing as people know more than what they say. Unsurpassed communication implies more than the ability to read, write and speak. People must be trained to listen and encouraged to take initiative and leadership roles targeting on increasing the worker's effectiveness and maximizing their potential. Effective communication is critical to the success of a company since transformation and creativity are only possible if working collaboratively across the business through of effective networking.

In Figures 9 and 10 contrasting philosophies are illustrated. Figure 9 illustrates Taylor's theory that management who have a tendency to be autocratic has all the intelligence, imagination and ideas critical to get the work done. The workers are simply the tools who will respond to their wishes to get the product(s) or service(s) out. Taylor would never accept the possibility that workers might possess the awareness, skills and competencies fundamental to perform their tasks without control and direction. He believed only a downward and outward movement of intellect connecting management at the upper level and the employees at the lower level was possible.

Taylor's Scientific Management Theory

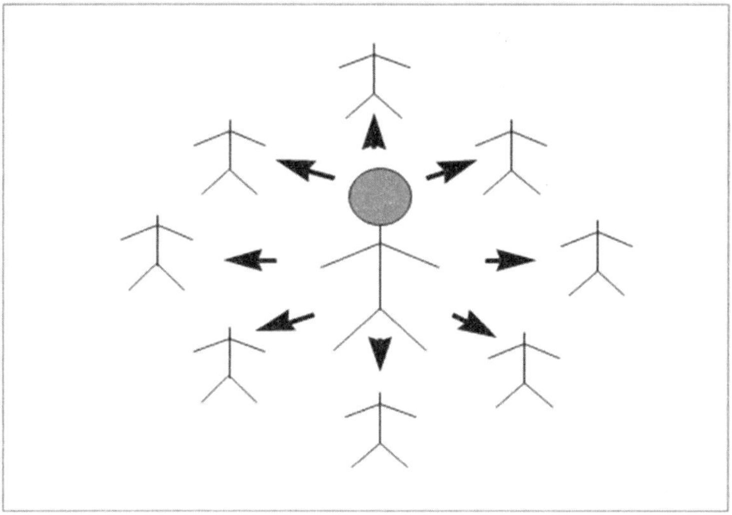

Figure 9

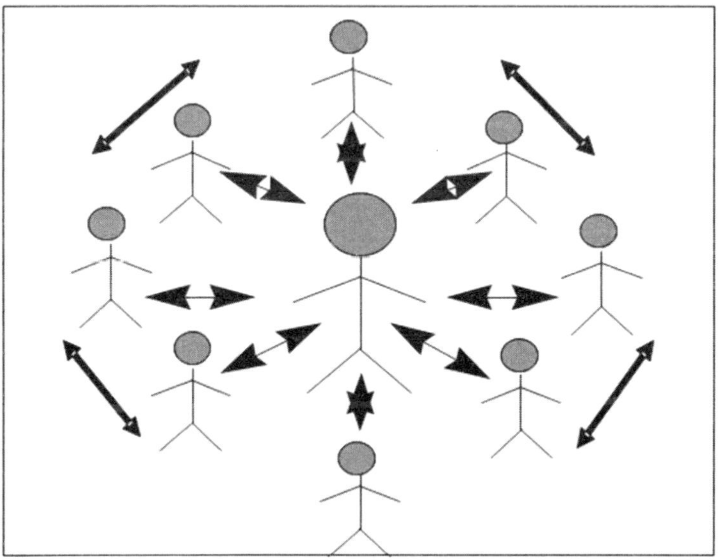

Figure 10

Human capital is dependent on relationships, and it is through them that workers develop human capital. Relationships are a primary source of credibility that help in generating, human capital, how it can be created and shared among others because this is where what they know is found when it is needed. Figure 10 illustrates a reshaping of the traditional corporate composition to one transformed to directing attention to the strategies of mass collaboration. The relationship demonstrates openness among the workforce, allowing for added opportunities for collaboration between workers, and the workers to and from management instead of competition among the workforce. The suggested format will help with eliminating fear in the workplace and creating an environment where workers are stimulated to utilize their minds and enjoy working in a highly productive, innovative and creative manner. Without social networks performance suffers.

A company's effort to leverage its human capital will always be a work in progress, an undertaking central to promoting a framework for the creation and understanding of new learning. Since the majority of learning comes from socialization, the process must promote and support relationships where individuals functioning in surroundings promoting socialization will meet challenges with excitement, enthusiasm and creativity.

Without workers, organizations do not exist. Without continual learning by the workers, the organizations will not be able to meet the 21st century global marketplace. Without a partnering relationship between the workers and the organization, neither will change. Without change, both will fail.

Chapter 6

Developing a Human Capital Management Culture

American corporations are experiencing turbulent change, necessitating a new type of labor force to triumph. William Bridges[1] explains a job in the new corporation is no longer an applicable concept. He states that *today's organization is rapidly being transformed from a structure built out of jobs, to a field of work needing to be done.* The attitude, giving an organization an *edge* is a level of confidence separating it from the competition and one that will determine success or failure in all decision faced.

Futurists suggest that in time *knowledge workers* will need to allocate up to 20% of their working day learning just to remain current with the awareness needs of the business. If this is to be accomplished, a major effort providing alternative methods for workers to learn will be important. Electronic classrooms, information networks, distant learning, interactive and multi-media systems etc., are already in large demand.

Today's workforce has become increasingly dissatisfied and believe the pleasure of work has been taken away from them and they are searching for answers, role models, feelings of security and a sense of loyalty. Employees appreciate being a part of a company with stimulating visions, purposeful missions and systems aligned to satisfy their needs for recognition, esteem and an opportunity for self-actualization.

Culture Cultivation

The term *Culture* is derived from Latin referring to the cultivation of the soil whereas the root of culture implies growth in a supportive environment. Therefore, changing and shaping a person's culture comes about owing to the cultivation of their mind through awareness. It is this cultivation of thoughts and ideas that adds merit to the organization's functioning and is central to why a competitor's method of doing business cannot be replicated. The culture in each company is unique as each is an activity of analysis, understanding and functioning within a particular setting. Although companies have intensified their efforts to attaining and sustaining an advantage, behavior has become central to change for the reason that it is through behavior that performance is altered. Behavior is contingent on human capital, which defines an organization's culture.

A good deal of research has gone into studying the success of Southwest Airlines and trying to determine why the other airlines are not able to duplicate its success, even after attempting to copy their operating methods. The fallacy of the assumption that successful modification will come simply by replicating the methodology used by Southwest Airlines in managing its resources and people, it is that they operate under a unique operating culture. Those that have attempted to copy it have never taken the time to really understand it, let alone their own culture and have all failed. A company's ability to serve, respond quickly and offer continuity of service to its customers is the corollary of internal processes and capability natural to their setting and operating model. Although Southwest pays less than other airlines the company experiences a higher number of applicants for open positions (over 150,000 for 5,000 jobs yearly), less absenteeism and employee mobility. Their difference is in the workplace, where employee interests are put above everything else. Management proactively introduces policies to motivate their workers, and keep the members excited about their jobs and believing in the company. Southwest's tactic is what customers see, want to hear and go out of their way to fly them. Customers envious of the working atmosphere like to hear that the company has approximately 800 married couples working for them, and management helps and will work where help is needed, regardless of whether it is ticketing, baggage handling, cleaning, etc. Southwest has proven that the ultimate outcome of treating workers with respect translates to lower costs and greater revenues. It is unfortunate, but there are rumors that the airline has changes its mode of operation with the change in upper management and the workforce is no longer as contented.

Corporate Cultural Readiness

The ultimate meaning of human capital is in its quality as an effect of its application. Critical practices fostering knowledge sharing or exchange are created through contributor recognition. Business systems, organizations and management methods have remained unyielding and resistant to change as demonstrated by Frederick Taylor's Scientific Management theory[3], which is still taught in graduate school. For continued existence a corporate setting that will alter management's mental capacity, habits of decision-making and learning must be created; something often taken as an act of faith. A corporate culture can be an inspiration when it possesses attributes that help in guiding the organization in the direction it has set. It is also the glue that holds it together in determining an open and supportive environment. The phrase *the way we do things around here,* is often heard as describing an company's culture, but in examining how they function, a better reading might be, *if this is the way things are done, then we should stop, because it is not working.*

People have become the most critical element in business and their value system is what places them above all else. For an organization to work collaboratively and effectively a common set of values and beliefs is essential to insure the information and knowledge shared is acceptable to all parties. Understanding an organization's cultural social norms and practices will help in incorporating them, but today's labor force appears to be disillusioned with the work environment. The workforce is continually asked to analyze their valued beliefs and become uncomfortable when forced to change. The outcomes are distressing; workers have become less cooperative, productive and object to having to contribute to a setting they oppose and consequently, may move to another company in hopes of finding the ideal. Workers have come to believe that today's business is meant to generate consequence only for the owners and shareholders, often by questionable methods. It is essential therefore, that values and deeds promoting trust, collaboration, flexibility and other key qualities are instilled into this world of transformation. These forces form an illustration of reality for the individuals, something that evolves to become the basis for how an organization will be developed and organized. Unfortunately, society appears to be moving from a community-based background centered on common shared values, morals and beliefs formed in the home, school, community and society as one, to an individualistic based system. Understandably it is the diverse corporate practices that help shape an organization's traditions and contribute to an individual's beliefs.

The Pursuit of Collaboration

Synergy occurs when the whole is greater than its parts, inferring 1 + 1 = 3. This exponential growth comes about when two individuals work to uncover an idea that is enhanced further than either individual could attain alone. Much like a sheet of plywood, collaboration is crucial to creating strength. The strength of an assembled sheet of plywood exceeds the combined strength of the separate wood elements from its composition. The sheet does not illustrate a compromise, but a new and better solution, one by which organizations can identify, capture, leverage and apply their understanding in solving problems.

Another example is a world-class symphony composed of individuals who individually might not be the best musicians, but when collaborating and functioning as a member of a group is regarded as the best. As a collective system the symphony is a dynamic organism by which patterns of meanings emerge, coordination flows, creativity, innovation and inspiration interact. Then by way of cross-fertilization the musicians excel by repeated exchange, feeding and growing upon one another. This collaborative concept is gradually gaining converts and as an upshot is developing a setting of improved efficiency and job satisfaction. In essence, collaboration has become the catalyst in changing work practices and experiences where workers see themselves possessing wherewithal worth sharing. The new economies of scale are based on the ability of the assorted distributed units to collaborate by sharing human capital. These characteristics are only possible if the attitude to life is one where all workers have respect, are empowered to contribute, committed, motivated and encouraged to make choices and possess an initiative to participate in as a team-player.

Organizational performance is subject not only on the intellectual attributes of the individuals who make up the organizations, but also by means of the many social relationships developed in the organization. Knowing who has what knowledge and understanding the networking, relationships and personalities involved will help in developing productive team efforts. In examining the associations of competition, cooperation and collaboration, the following table illustrates the differences.

	Competition	**Cooperation**	**Collaboration**
Power	Experienced	Balanced	Shared
Outcomes	Win-Lose	Win-Win	Win-Win

Deming's theory of Profound Knowledge has been credited with helping improve performance, productivity, quality and organizational effectiveness. Deming[3] believed management, workers and the community would live better materially and spiritually if his philosophy was followed. His theory emphasizes the importance of supporting one's desire to learn and direct all familiarity not only to things known, but to broadening one's learning in other disciplines. It was his belief that without a unique management system, one focusing on the human elements, American companies would be challenged in mounting a reckoning force for the global marketplace.

To be successful with any alteration will require knowing the value it intends to provide and to whom. This is especially true when changing from a system of competition to one of collaboration as opposed to management by conflict. *Collaboration* is possibly the foundation element supporting the spirit of a *Win-Win* setting and not a *Win-Lose* environment. A *Win-Win* setting brings together a genuine teamwork where all parties are of a similar frame of mind and constantly striving to achieve an effect where each is a winner. Deming's theory states that a conversion from the mistaken belief that competition is inherently good for the enterprise, employees and customers, to the realization that collaboration working for the mutual benefit of society has greater potential.

Another foundation element in the Deming theory is *motivation.* He claims modern management has stolen and smothered the workforce's dignity and removed enjoyment from their work. Intrinsic motivation is vital if the workforce is going to experience broad-scale improvement, but its absence in the workplace has helped workers lose their innate dignity, self-esteem and empathy for others. Motivation is not enough to ensure a knowledge social order. To guarantee such a method employees must participate in the leveraging and sharing of awareness and this will require motivational methods to be built into the work process. Employees should be motivated to share knowledge, but before they will, they have to understand that sharing enables them to work more effectively and will lead to personal development and recognition. Since knowledge is useful when action is encouraged, any exchange will enable employees to sharpen their analytical, communications and interpersonal skills. Knowledge sharing helps in reducing the anxiety of losing job security and generating a desire to share what is known. This aids in lessening the costly effort of having to function independently and eliminates the feeling of selfishness, lack of motivation and continual search for payback; wondering "*what's in it for me?*"

Significant talent loss may hinder and create an atmosphere where intellect simply seeps out of the door and is not available to generate innovative ideas or solutions. This is critical when people leave one company for another and take trade secrets or competencies, which may possibly be shared and provide more immediate use and solutions elsewhere. Sharing one's realization and abilities is based on a cause and effect process; if workers believe they are a part of a process where their input is valuable and will be accepted, they will willingly share. If this is not the case barriers of opposition are put in place. Management must understand the need to make personnel responsible only to themselves. In this manner they will work to learn, and then go on to sow and harvest new intellect and learning.

Ethical Issues

A business setting characterized by exorbitant management salaries, reductions in personnel and the lack of social responsibilities is obliged to question its moral obligations not only to its workers, but also the community. During the last two decades, the values of loyalty, honesty, trust, integrity, respect and devotion all appear to have disappeared. Claiming, *our workers are our most valuable asset*; coined by countless organizations, is not believed by many of the workers as they feel they are only paid lip service and little is done to substantiate regard for them. Management's lack of understanding of a worker's actual worth to the success of the company often results in a reluctance or unwillingness to make the fundamental investments necessary for the workforce to remain competitive, all while the value of their cognitive skills is becoming greater and more valuable. The new emphasis on human capital may be changing the situation however, as business leaders have developing greater awareness of how difficult it is to re-train, re-educate, and re-create lost awareness. As well as looking for innovative ways to help their personnel locate the expertise needed.

Once the leaders in Research and Development spending American companies now fall behind many foreign ones such as Toshiba and Sony, today's leaders in R&D, which can be seen by their success. If U.S. corporations are to regain their leadership strengths, the workforce must be deemed a strategic asset rather than a cost and be managed dynamically to make the most of its human capital. This effort will require:

- understanding what drives worker efficiency

- redesigning jobs and organizational structures that will improve quality, reduce costs and increase productivity
- training, developing and acquiring the talent needed
- ensuring that people at all levels have the competencies, desire and values to perform to their best; and
- creating a workplace mode that encourages excellence, collaboration and staff retention.

Millions of workers have become disgusted and distrustful of management by its seemingly unethical, uncaring acts of greed, and companies that have encountered ethical problems may never recover. One such example involves Al "*Chainsaw*" Dunlap, an ex-CEO of Sunbeam[4] who believed that to be a winner a company had to concentrate on improving its bottom-line quickly and developed a reputation for being ruthless because of his methods for reducing costs by plunging his workforce. In promoting shareholder's interests Dunlap did away with all charitable activities and eliminated any social responsibility the company may have had. Eventually his methods although not illegal, suggested ethically suspicious company financials when reported. He was ultimately ousted by the board of directors and subsequently sued. Consequently, Sunbeam never reached the status it once held before Dunlap's stewardship and was eventually taken over by the Jarden Corporation after filing for bankruptcy in 2001.

Another example is where four of the top paid executives in Arizona in 2002 worked for ON, a distribution company spun off by Motorola. Although the workforce had been trimmed, remaining worker's had their pay and benefits cut, and were forced to take unpaid vacations, while the ON executives themselves received large bonuses. This was an example of those worthy of greater rewards not receiving them, while those who deserved the least were given the most. Seeing that management was not sharing the pain did little to help in motivating ON's workers. It was later suggested by an outside consulting firm that ON's employee remuneration should be reinstated due to the negative impressions of the company perceived by the community. ON has since decided to move their operations to Malaysia.

Management fearful for their jobs, often regard the employee as the enemy, and some have acted unethically, leading to scandals and lawsuits such as those with Enron, Tyco, Siemens, World-Com, Cendant and more recently financial institutions such as Lehman Brothers, Citigroup, AIG, and others. Even more disturbing and disgusting examples illustrating the lack of concern for employees bring to mind Enron. A good deal has been written about the company's actions and until recently with the Madoff Ponzi case this might have been remembered as the most unethical business practice of all time. Enron's management was aware of what was occurring with the business, and while preventing the employees from withdrawing funds from their 401K savings were themselves withdrawing approximately $1B. Even more disturbing was the fact that management hid the information of their receiving bonuses for the preceding year that would have given approximately $13,500 to each of the four thousand employees who lost their jobs and savings. Ironically, if one would have gone to the Enron website a sixty-four page document describing the company's core values would be presented; emphasizing ethics and esteem for one another. It appears to have been a set of rules meant for the employees, but not management, and the end does not appear to be in sight. Even with the adverse publicity of this company unethical practices continue along with recent charges to different financial institution, and automotive leaders.

The three CEO's of General Motors, Ford and Chrysler recently flew to Washington to meet with Congress in their separate private jets to request an initial $25 Billion bailout loan. Maybe even more disturbing was the fact they had no idea or plan what would have to be done to survive as viable enterprises, and in a setting where thousands of workers were let go these three supposed leaders initially stated an unwillingness to reduce their eight to ten figure salaries.

Although management's compensation and perks continue to increase at a turbo-charged pace, studies by About. Com: Management show management's salaries for 2000 were 581 times that of the hourly worker and bonuses increasing at a higher rate and still climbing. While management's compensation has continued to sky-rocket the workers continue to lose. Many have cut or eliminated retirement benefits, matching funds, tuition reimbursement, insurance, health benefits and reduced vacation time for their workers and retirees. Some have switched entire non-exempt groups to exempt status so overtime wouldn't have to be paid, yet expect the workforce to work additional hours referred to as casual overtime. Others workers have had their wages cut when their work hours are shortened and or extended with no increase in salary. Companies such as United Airlines, Delta and others no longer contribute to their employee's pensions and some such as Polaroid have reduced or cut off all pension checks without notice. Perks such as coffee; bottled water, pizzas on Friday's and anything else that might have initially been intended to help motivate the workers have been abolished by most companies. Still others are removing the quality of Work-Life Balance programs initially established to help personnel address stress, depression, and anxiety, which are supposedly principle to today's working environment.

Especially detrimental to the workplace is perhaps what some companies such as Circuit City exercised. Circuit City fired 3500 of its higher paid personnel, in order to replace them with others or even the same individuals let go at lower salaries. It was my initial belief this unethical action by management would ultimately influence productivity negatively due to the lack of customer-focus by the remaining employees. Fear for their jobs, and a lack of concern for the workforce eventually contributed to Circuit City going bankrupt and out of business. It should be mentioned that the compensation of six of Circuit City's top executives averaged $33.5 Million during the last three years whereas the average salary for those let go was less than $15 an hour.

Another unethical example is Robert Nardelli's decision as CEO of Home Depot to replace most of the full-time staff with part-timers. The outcome was an inexperienced workforce with little understanding to support the company's core competency, and a lost of prominence the company once had in the home improvement business. It is a well known fact that when with GE, Nardelli was referred to as *Little Jack,* named after Jack Welch who was known as *Neutron Jack.* Welch had a reputation for getting rid of all the employees and only leaving a building. The irony of Nardelli's actions was that Lowe's, Home Depot's competitor, hired many of the knowledgeable experienced employees let go and experienced a tremendous growth due to improved customer-focus, while Home Depot experienced a loss.

Another unethical case is with management's false promises. Companies are taken over with the CEO promising no modification and then doing something different. One such example involves GE. When the company acquired RCA, Jack Welch then CEO promised the RCA employees nothing would change from this action but, within six months RCA was completely decimated and thousands of jobs were lost. Still another example of ill promises involves Monsanto, whose CEO promised no amendment in benefits when the company branched off to form another entity, yet did just the opposite. The peculiar aspect of all of these decisions is that the Federal government supposedly supports these dealings through tax credits; in essence actually encouraging these actions. This deteriorating focus to employees only contributes to an organization's culture characterized by a lack of collaboration, diminished innovation, lack of customer-focus, and increased resistance to change.

The ethical issues don't end with the business world as it is becoming evident in the academic arena and the field of Sports. In sports, more and more unsportsmanlike conduct, such as cheating, maiming of competitors, and taking of steroids is experienced. The sad aspect of these actions appears to be accepted, giving the message that this is appropriate conduct to our young. Because of the requirements *No-Child Left Behind* has imposed on education, requiring students to pass unmistakable testing levels, teachers across the U.S. have been found to be misreporting student scores and even changing them to indicate positive effects.

Human Capital Context

The underlying driver for the attainment and use of knowledge is helping to solve problems and make satisfactory decisions by hopefully identifying who has the particular knowledge and their location. How human capital is interpreted and used characterizes a context that may be explicit or unseen, but regardless of which, a human capital system requires that everyone is able to interpret and identify intellect in the same manner and arrive at the same conclusions. All organizations have basic measurements in common (e.g. headcount, absenteeism rates, employee turnover), but there is no standard set of measures for everyone to use. Every organization differs in the ways in which they identify, use and disseminate their key measures, and what is important in one context might be less relevant in another.

The principal challenge involves the sharing of human capital and its accuracy in communicating what others know in order to match what is currently shared to precise processes. Overall, the sharing process can be reduced to a common method of forming, combining and understanding the concept of learning and its context in using human capital appropriately. Having the ability to use concepts instead of simply words is an improved ability used in solving problems and making fitting choices. In its most simplistic sense, context corresponds to one's analysis and communication of the situations presented. This requires focusing on the meaning of words, not the words themselves. The use of concepts is only possible with the understanding and shaping of a worker's actions as an outcome of comprehension. It is most important therefore, that an organization develop shared operational definitions, standardized measurements and improved learning about the context function, which would allow intellect to be shared.

Incentives and Rewards

Some believe an incentive system will help in defining the relationship of sharing knowledge in an organization. Still others believe that with the right environment there is no need to bribe workers to obtain their participation for improving or changing performance. At the end of the day, all personnel want to learn, express their creativity and innovative abilities, offer suggestions, and ideas contributing to decision-making and solving problems. The general culture in American business however, appears to demand so much from its people in that it hampers the sharing of any of these actions, and does not suggest giving incentives or rewards to those workers at the lower levels. If there are incentives however, the emphasis might best be to reward a team or group versus solely individual efforts. Both the sharer(s) and receiver(s) of knowledge should be rewarded on the bases of value creation of sustainable improvements and the development of operational capabilities. This would require that those with the knowledge are willing to share this awareness in order that it can be applied, re-used and even expanded. To succeed will require a process that celebrates those involved, and a focus on the human aspects that determine the capabilities available, and a management system to achieve them.

Many organizations are in a state of flux, often creating a system of turmoil, anxiety and even chaos. They appear unable to focus in one direction because they are being pulled in so many others. Management suffers by not learning from their mistakes and seemingly just *fires* at crucial organizational transformation without first taking aim at what should be done to be successful, which will require personal makeover. Practice has shown that successful conversion is stimulated by a clear alignment to objectives, on top of having the knowledge and understanding of how performance can be improved. For this reason it is vital that organizations persevere, and perform suitable due diligence when making decisions. Firms working to create a supportable workplace must be willing to take risks, and relinquish or modify bad habits in order to learn from their mistakes.

A major challenge in the human capital effort is the development of a process that will force on the optimum reuse of specific knowledge. Such a process will allow an organization to do what it does more rapidly without the continual need to recreate more. By way of a common direction people can look at their setting, expectations and work to develop an optimum process, supporting reclaim with knowledge transferring efforts. Although critical and fundamental, it is imperative to look at what and how something is accomplished. It is impossible to learn something simply by reading a book or listening to others. To learn it, one has to study it, spend time with it and get to know it. The understanding and management of human capital on the other hand is fundamental in allowing for reprocessing and sharing efforts.

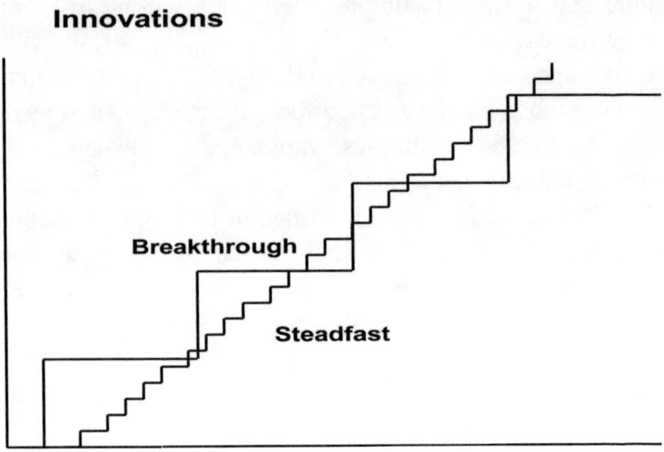

Figure 11

Much as knowledge and economic results are interconnected so to can an organization's culture and performance affect its economic success. For this reason, drastic change in driving the rapid development of skills and competencies to meet needs must come about. Figure 11 illustrates two methods by which ideas can bring meaning to an organization. The methods are breakthrough innovation, usually the effect of a major action, such as a technological conversion like implementing a more powerful computer system to provide greater capability and dedicated growth to the organization. It is the smaller but unwavering incremental innovative growth schemes that hold the real strength. These continuous efforts and actions require less effort, and fewer resources to implement, but the workers are more involved. The dedicated efforts by the workers help expand an organization's ability to detect trends, and create products and services to meet the demand. The ideal situation would be to align the two methods into a more powerful force.

Globalization – Do we have the means?

With globalization believed critical to sustain growth, companies now attempt to compete in the international and domestic arenas; both requiring quicker and improved decision-making technology. Few however, have learned the necessity of functioning in an international way of life. The lack of standardization, inflexibility, misunderstanding, and language are obstacles preventing cooperation across global boundaries. As a whole, American companies believe they are functioning in a global setting, but I believe this is far from the truth. In many situations, and the appearance given is that counterparts in other countries must function in the American mode or they are at fault. Business processes are put in place without validating whether or not it is possible to function in the diverse surroundings of other countries. An example involves the use of cellular telephones. A colleague lost his cellular phone between flights in a United States airport. Realizing its loss when he arrived at his destination in South America, he attempted to reach the telephone provider's customer support group to deactivate the phone. The only number he could locate in his user guide was an 800 number, which did not function when called from outside of the United States. After an intensive search, he was able to locate the phone number of the store where he had purchased the telephone and on calling the store the sales personnel helped in locating the number he needed to call in order to disable his telephone. When the American airline companies introduced e-tickets I can remember criticizing them when I was turned back from customs in Buenos Aires, Argentina and then again in London, UK because I didn't have a hard copy of my ticket.

For human capital to be a productive force in a global marketplace will require participation in a community where cultural forces interact in shaping a future and where workers in the 21st Century understand the business dynamics and cultural atmosphere. A major challenge will require developing an elevated level of awareness where the employee is able to communicate within the context of a turbulent global setting. This will require the development of a new and different tactic through a supporting infrastructure sustaining a long-term vision. The greatest opportunity for success lies in the building of organizations on existing forte, and working on the void in the workforce to improve the method in which they work.

Success Breeds Complacency

American companies appear to have become arrogant, complacent and unwilling to alter cultural habits. Habitually, they are programmed to throw money at problems, looking for the quick mend, and do not realize that money is not the determining criteria. People are not always motivated by money, but by a desire to excel, allowed to contribute, have ownership to achieve, and make a difference.

In today's environment American businesses lack three attributes, *persistence, patience*, and *perseverance*. Where *patience* is the art of waiting, *persistence*, the art of being stubborn, can lead to making the impossible real, and *perseverance*, the third attribute, is the ability to stay focused and have an unwavering tenacity to remove the obstacles to success. As a unit, these three traits become the strength of endurance, something today's leaders appear to lack. This is often seen in the results from the many corporate systems introduced in the last twenty-five years. Lacking patience will often direct someone off target, leading them to make incorrect decisions, resulting in negative outcomes. Persistence, working in conjunction with patience will help keep people directed to a vision requiring attention. Combining these two traits with perseverance will help in keeping them directed to a mental picture. This can be seen when examining Total Quality Management (TQM). Few enterprises attempted to implement the philosophy for the reason that it was said to require at least 20 years; in essence a generation to completely transform it into an operating culture. Some that did attempt to implement the TQM process may have attempted other business wide transformations, which may have also failed miserably due to their lack of perseverance. When implementing a new methodology, cynicism is one outcome that often follows failure, and may even contribute to the increase in cost and resources making the next attempt more problematic.

There has literally been an unknown number of dissimilar management systems implemented over the last 40 years. At enormous expense and resource utilization, corporations and management like sheep, moved to these methodologies in apprehension that their competitors may have found the ultimate cure. In no chronological order and far from a complete list; methodologies such as: Management By Objectives (MBO), Theories X and Y, Matrix Organization, Total Quality Management (TQM), Continuous Process Improvement, Team-Building, Organizational Learning, Re-engineering, Systems Thinking, ISO-9000 Certification, Risk Management, Strategic Planning, Supply Chain Management, Lean thinking, Knowledge Management, Customer Relationship Management, Down-sizing, the Seven Habits philosophy, and Human Capital are some examples, and now I am hearing tones of a one referred to as Design Innovation.

Regardless of the system, each advocates the importance of process improvement benefits, and implementations have resulted in gains in the short-term. In most situations, short sightedness has caused many of the companies that implemented these methodologies to experience limited success in their long-term efforts. Their short-term emphasis often lacks sustainability and after a period any benefit gained was lost and the methodology was later deemed a fad. After a methodology is introduced, new ideas generated often lead to anxiety and a dread of risking difference. This constant changing often leads to neophobia; an anxiety of newness which often has a major affect on a company's ability to adapt or transform in an appropriate manner. One might even question why continual amendment that brings disharmony, frustration, doubt and confusion is introduced. Corporate leaders never initiate more than one program at a time, and when they move on, so do the promoters of the particular initiative.

Under all of these methodologies, programs have been introduced to hopefully give some type of identity, build a sense of unity, and hopefully promote something to believe in. "*We make the difference*," "*Fly the friendly Skys of United*," "*Ford is a better idea*," "*We bring things to life*," "*The people make the difference,*" are some examples. Unfortunately, the effect is often an illusion, some element needing investigation because it is meant to set an idea in motion to make the company more favorable. As an example a company will experience an increase in business upwards of 15% if it states it provides quality service. Unless it does, this increase is only temporary, similar to any methodology introduced. All too often, management is perceived as coming from traditional ways and engineering-based thinking; Scientific Management, a task-oriented process is an example. Management continues to wonder why the results desired are not achieved, little realizing they are forcing new ideas through the use of old perceptions and tools. It comes down to the human capital a company can capture and utilize.

I sometimes wonder how all of the education, training, consultation as well as the numerous articles and books written about the management discipline available can generate so little effective conversion. New management efforts are often doomed to failure since one of the major traps they fall into is their inability to learn. In much the same way that the emphasis the quality movement has had to develop towards knowledge and human capital, management and organizations must undergo a fundamental modification of values and beliefs. Any transformation requires that there be a moral, ethical and spiritual accountability while directing attention to satisfying a theory that introduces a new paradigm where everybody wins. Consequently, business leaders are to be held accountable for embodying the elements of this major cultural shift.

A company's success often leads to overconfidence and self-satisfaction while lessening flexibility and responsiveness. An example is Henry Ford refusing to introduce a color other than black even when he was losing market share to other automobile manufacturers. He produced only black automobiles until the 1940's and had lost a large portion of the market share he had held earlier.

Organizations should take a systematic, proactive slant in looking for methods to restructure their human capital strategies in directing efforts to the global marketplace. It often appears that the methods used by management to achieve productivity gains seemingly push their targets further out of reach. All methods appear to encompass two directions; first, reducing direct labor; and second, the addition of new technology, both used with little realization that things do not improve simply by doing more of the same, or wanting it good enough. There must be a realization that a different strategic line of attack is needed to produce greater effective results.

Strategic Transformation

While the ultimate goal is organizational effectiveness with fitting management and communications the key drivers; it is imperative that management set the context for the human capital process with flexible and responsive knowledge-enabled workers through strategic planning. The strategic management process should include a complete set of actions important for an organization to achieve high functioning effectiveness. Strategic human resource planning is an integral part of human capital management and development, requiring an understanding and close coordination across all distributed sources in order to achieve the most appropriate personnel mix. Such planning helps to ensure an organization is staffed with the requisite skill sets and competencies for developing future leaders. These proactive actions will require the organization to: (1) introduce a visualization enlightening its existence and what is central to satisfy its associated objectives; (2) evaluate the background in order to understand its opportunities and threats; (3) analyze its strengths and weaknesses, before implementing actions to improve its processes and moving beyond its means; (4) identify and understand the basic learning needed to implement the strategy defined; (5) implement the best alternatives; and (6) validate each individual's skills and capabilities.

Management must amend how they perceive their personnel. One of the most annoying issues workers complain about is being monitored during work. In many facilities cubicle walls are installed desk high so the people can be monitored. Scott Adams[6] an artist who has become successful with his series of Dilbert cartoons highlighting stories office workers share about their cubicle experiences. Impressions given are that managers must always be in control and appear to be waiting for the workers to make a mistake, something inevitable, and then later reprimanding them for it. If workers are fearful of making mistakes they will not take risks and attempt anything new. Another annoyance is management not listening when workers offer or make suggestions. I realize it is possible I am generalizing, but during 40 years of corporate life in a variety of settings I have often experienced and witnessed this situation. Management is often aloof and not personable, never seeming to have time to expend with their staff – something is always more important. When meeting with employees they will answer the telephone or look for an excuse to do something else if the conversation is deemed too long. This is the same management that states they have an open door policy where all are welcome to go in and converse. Ultimately, employees quit trying to communicate and share. My conclusion is that as a whole, management lacks the skills needed for listening to and understanding those for whom they are responsible.

The ideas of bygone times have an everlasting quality. Involving the workforce in a shared vision, sharing a common goal, in a creative tradition will help produce a labor force that is committed, innovative, creative and one that leverages individual intellect to improve performance and productivity. One of the major problems organizations face when introducing change is leadership. In many instances management is seen as lacking vision as to *where* the organization is going, *how* it will arrive there and *what* needs to be done to make it. The lack of a road map extends the impression that little guidance exists and employees become confused as to what is expected of them. Leaders in the information age need to encourage an atmosphere where the workers are open and willing to comment and one that will help them exercise an ability to promote value for the organization. They require the inspiration to care for the needs of their employees by supporting, guiding and stimulating those who struggle and demonstrating an interest in success. In addition, the leaders can then look to their own requirements and be seen participating much like tribal chiefs who always ensured all members of the tribe had eaten before taking food themselves. If a leader should leave the organization and the individuals remaining can't say they are better, then he or she has failed.

As with all management methodologies, effective use of human capital is no different. It starts at the top of the organization where the linking of a shared-vision begins. Management must *walk the talk*, *practice what they preach* and *lead by example*. Only in this manner will the regard needed to possibly motivate the workforce be earned. As a discipline, human capital management uses an organization's human capital and social networks as powerful levers for innovation and growth in increasing organizational effectiveness. This can be accomplished by managing the freedom and autonomy of individuals, provided the workers have a mental picture of what they can focus on, be totally committed in doing what must be done to reach the desired end. This will require a strategic plan, with the technological and proper outlooks to help provide the ability to interact effectively with management and other organizations.

Another requirement might be a reward and incentive process to recognize personnel for the success of their efforts. The irony of this proposal is that although it is inexpensive to put into place, it is something most management shirks from. Changing culture is resource consuming and requires leadership to articulate a forward thinking vision with the realization that workers cannot satisfy the business proposals by themselves. It is the leader's duty to become gatekeepers and champions of the corporate agenda and develop plans to match its competencies and resources the marketplace demands. To fully develop a learning organization an effective use of the resources required is critical. An organization's ability to focus on the potency of others in building excellence is of fundamental importance. Mastery in jobs, professions or activities is verified in action, execution and conduct; not just in awareness. A company's customs must be linked to its outcomes, which can be realized if measures are a part of the process. This will necessitate that the needed resources, to insure the workforce has the required development and technology are provided.

Knowledge is Vital to Successful Mergers

The travesty of mergers is the realization that in many situations the management of the company pushing for a merger is often having difficulty in operating their current enterprise. It does not end there however, for the reason that the company being merged with may also be experiencing problems. Management of both companies seem to believe they can resolve the problems and do better with the merger, but it often results in a larger company with a bigger problem. One of the many examples was the merger between Compaq and DEC – Digital Equipment Corporation. Both corporations were having trouble, but believed they would survive and grow by merging. A few years later Compaq merged again, this time with HP – Hewlett-Packard. More recent examples involve banks. The Bank of America had a record of acquiring other banks and ultimately had to obtain a $138 Billion bailout after acquiring Merrill Lynch, Country-Wide, and US Trust in what many analysts claimed were moves to build Ken Lewis' (CEO) reputation. And now BA is seeking additional monies to stay afloat. Citigroup, another financial group also has a history of acquiring other banks and was banned by the Federal Reserve in 2005 because of these actions due to a concern of their ability to remain solvent. Unfortunately, once the ban was lifted they proceeded to acquire additional banks and now after an initial bailout of $45 Billion they are requesting additional funds to remain solvent. The interesting aspect regarding the bailouts is that the U.S. government will basically have ownership in these financial groups, something President Andrew Jackson feared would happen and fought against during his two terms over 175 years ago.

AT&T is just another example of unsuccessful mergers and takeovers. Many of its mergers or acquisitions have seemingly all been failures (NCR, just one). Another example involved the Federated retail stores. After several mergers and acquisitions the company went bankrupt. If we examine Chrysler's account on mergers we would see where their first merger involved the Dodge Company, then American Motors was acquired, followed by Daimler (Mercedes-Benz) purchasing of the company, and now with even greater problems they are discussing merging with Fiat. It doesn't end there as it has continually occurred in the airline industry and now we see where Northwest Airlines and Delta and America West and US Airlines all companies with major problems merging with others. These are examples of where growth for growths sake may not be the best route in today's milieu. It appears the only winners are the management of the company taken over, who usually leave with multi-million dollar severance packages.

Most mergers are evaluated in financial concerns with little thought of the criteria that the success of the merger should be based upon. No one appears to consider the: (1) lack of a common vision under which the companies should align themselves to common strategic initiatives; (2) need for a united setting where management has an understanding of the different traditions in each of the organizations in order to determine a plan of action to removing barriers and obstacles; and (3) human capital strength determined by means of an assessment of the different levels and execution disparities in the organizations that need to be merged in order to define a corrective plan for resolution. One of the biggest problems is the lack of due diligence to determine and to understand what needs to be accomplished in order to be successful. This would require employee involvement, something seldom encouraged.

Another contributor to the cultural problems in today's workplace and quite possibly the major contributor is the enormous widespread mismatch in salaries between the average worker and the CEO. What was a ratio of 15 – 20 times in the 1970's has augmented to what many believe to be

600 times or more coming into the 21st century. In 1991 when President George H. W. Bush took a number of American company's CEO's to Japan to discuss trade restrictions a vast number of media covered this historic event where these business leaders would meet with their Japanese counterparts. What actually transpired was never shared with the public. The meeting in essence terminated with the first question presented by the Japanese. The Japanese leaders stated that the salary ratio between Japan's highest level executives and the lowest level worker was 17 times and asked the American CEO's what the ratio of compensation was between them and their lowest level workers. There was no response from the American leaders, but it was later determined to be over 500 times. The idea of asking for trade restrictions became fruitless. I have often wondered if upon hearing this is what made President Bush get sick on the Prime Minister of Japan. Present disclosures from the auto corporations found the highest paid Japanese brand company CEO compensation was less than $1 Million while the CEOs of the Big 3 were paid many times more. This huge division in salaries and constant effort to cut costs by trimming down the workforce has contributed to the uncomfortable feeling of betrayal, that no one cares for them, and as workers they will never be rewarded for their labors. The effect of this discontentment is a lack of trust, diminished motivation and employee mobility, resulting in unplanned costs to recruit replacements and the loss of key resources, often never recovered.

Business must not motivate the labor force to behavior that will cause negative responses from conditioned stimulus. In the course of generalization the employees learn to stereotype creativity and innovation as a contributor to higher CEO benefits and negative responses for the workforce. Examples of extreme CEO remunerate and severance packages have really helped in increasing discontentment in the workforce since corporate reductions usually benefit senior management.

It is believed that Richard Fuld of Lehman Brothers received $500 Million, and Charles Prince, CEO of Citigroup received a $12.5 Million bonus while there was still money on hand before the enterprises took major financial hits as a result of Real Estate loans mismanagement. Robert Nardelli's recent departure from Home Depot came with a severance of $210 Million, United Health's CEO William McGuire received $1 Billion in total compensation, and Exxon's Lee Raymond received $405 Million are other examples of extreme severance packages, all given while staff was cut. Ironically, after being let go for not accomplishing what the shareholders wanted, these same individuals are often hired by other companies to seemingly do the same thing. After his departure from Home Depot, Nardelli took over Chrysler as CEO and was removed from this position when the company filed bankruptcy and did not receive a severance package.

Knowledge and human power are synonymous, since the ignorance of the first frustrates the effect.

Francis Bacon[1]

Chapter 7

Catch-up is Not a Game

To many European, Asian, and Canadian companies that have had human capital efforts in place for over 10 years, human capital is seen as a new era for understanding the contribution of individuals in the workplace and something increasingly critical to success. Directing a focus on the human capital emphasis is relatively new to American Companies, and such efforts appear to concern larger enterprises that have only had them in place for a short period. I have the impression that there is a belief that this is just another management fad to help consultancies sell their services. We have had some success however, because some are beginning to understand the importance of leveraging their human capital and are using technology to progress. One such enterprise, Hewlett-Packard (HP), developed a system identified as *Customer Service Knowledge Banks*. The system is comprised of a directory of experts and a repository of training aids that can be addressed by internal trainers. By cross-referencing ideas assembled from enterprise-wide human capital geographically located throughout the world collaborating and sharing, HP has determined real problems; in particular problems involving the interests and common good of the organization. In the HP system, vital attributes are defined and the individuals possessing them identified, located and correlated with their human capital for wider circulation. This system has proven to save time and has contributed to eliminating unnecessary training and education. British Petroleum (BP) is another company that has developed a system to help its worker's learn from earlier business conclusions. The desired effect is to identify what could be learned from decisions made that resulted in successes and failures and then using this information to formulate future judgments. The BP process has generated large savings and is just one example where evaluating attained awareness has produced enormous benefits.

The company that may have implemented the most successful human capital program might be IBM. Through the use of its Practitioner Portal system IBM has developed a repository of structured information which serves as the institutional memory throughout its global operations. IBM's system pulls together and captures information, the status of ongoing projects, knowledge and experiences. It also provides access to press releases, speeches and related materials from news services, all which can be retrieved throughout the company effectively and easily. One potential problem is perhaps in their attempt to amass as much understanding as possible, a system has been created that continues to grow in complexity and may soon become too complicated to manage. Although helpful to have technological applications in place to assist collaboration among employees, unless a proper practice is in the work environment it will not be successful.

It should be realized that not all of what an individual knows is available for immediate use, as knowledge possessed may not be available or functional when needed. Also, knowledge learned in one situation may not be applicable in another, and although relevant to still another situation, it may not be accessible. A more significant problem may be with the actual accessing of human capital. As stated, knowledge is private, and when learned or used emotions may come into play, requiring an understanding of what initiates the different emotion forms. Since no individual is an expert in everything it sometimes becomes fundamental to rely on the intelligence and expertise of others. Getting the right answer needed is not always simple unless one knows who may have the expertise desired and where they are located. Of greater importance is the need for upright working relationships to exist for the flow of any knowledge to be of any consequence. The sharing of any human capital may result in workers becoming sensitive to its reception for varied reasons.

Learning How to Learn

Nancy Dixon[2] compares the organizational learning cycle to Kolb's[3] experiential learning cycle, in which individuals generate ideas, integrate concepts, interpret ideas and then act accordingly. Dixon defines organizational learning as "...the intentional use of learning processes at the individual, group and system level to continuously transform the organization in a direction that is increasingly satisfying to its stakeholders." To flourish, companies must compete in attaining, sustaining and retaining those possessing the human capital crucial to remain competitive.

As human capital becomes critical to competition, the ability to learn becomes imperative in the race to win. Learning how to learn - the upper-most level of organizational learning - has become a requirement for the new workforce. Knowing how to learn implies that an individual will learn new competencies easier, which will be reflected in observable activities. Yet, it is not that simple. To learn, it is essential that one first learn how to learn. Having this ability, one can learn improved methods of learning how to learn best and the methods and format to use. Utilizing this realization will lead to greater creativity and innovation in dealing with the constant changing workplace is possible.

Before acquiring the knowledge and skills vital for

today's environment, many individuals need to use effective learning strategies. Knowing how to come by learning is definitely a skill more critical than the knowledge. Some of an individual's learning can occur in the workplace, but a critical prerequisite is that workers are taught how to attain knowledge before coming to the workplace. Individuals and organizations need to learn in order to make appropriate choices critical to solving problems. Workers must have the readiness to learn by means of aspiration, imagination, collaboration and experimentation. Since education is the key to using awareness effectively, learning can be linked to the situation by which knowledge develops. Following management's direction makes it mandatory that people accept accountability for learning in support of an organization's strategic initiatives.

Socialization as a Source of Human Capital

Montague[4] told us that *we get more of our beliefs from the testimony of our fellows than from any other source. Little of our knowledge of the universe is directly tested by our own intuition, reason, experience, or practice.* This may have been factual when he put these words to paper in 1925, but in today's setting, best practices, solving problems and decision-making are best defined utilizing individual intellect, expertise, intuition and reason in synergy with that of others. Learning attained and created from one's involvement is a major significance in the real world, and expands exponentially when coming together with others. It is believed that if individuals have a particular force such as earlier learning, they can prevail over ten others in guiding decision-making efforts. This becomes obvious when evaluating the outcomes from the television program *Who Wants to be a Millionaire.* When the candidate uses the audience for help, they are correct more than 90% of the time, but when using the so-called experts the %age drops to less than 65%. This is an example that illustrates the energy of many being able to disseminate human capital to maximize a person's intellect, while increasing their worth to the organization.

Employees learn when it is beneficial to them, and when to respond to what they know in helping satisfy their purpose, above all, that of achievement. An individual's effectiveness can be correlated to their intelligence and implies that a person can interpret, inquire and employ understanding to different situations while simultaneously generating more. In essence, individuals enjoying a greater access to learning often prove to be more effective, have the ability to make advanced decisions and can take quicker action. Consequently, additional learning may lead to an enhanced awareness, changed attitudes and belief that can be integrated into an employee's work. Experienced workers are obliged to become the organization's messengers; sharing human capital to improve the current situation like an ant colony, which is adaptive and responsive to any situation, where all members work to the common goal of accumulating food in order to survive.

A social relationship is only possible when functioning as a member of a team, leveraging and sharing abilities and knowledge for the benefit of the whole. It has repeatedly been proven that relationships, interactions and communication are best in a setting of honesty, trust and respect; something seen when observing Asian American students. Studies have determined that due to their socialization, propensity to share, and putting the collective interests of all ahead of their own, Asian Americans have superior grades over their non-Asian classmates, and are often the winners of prestigious educational scholarships. Asian Americans usually have a strong reliance on relationships based mainly on trust. They not only go to class and eat together they usually study as a group more than non-Asians.

We intensify our learning more effectively through experiential techniques such as dialogue or problem solving than by passive listening. It is in the course of dialogue that knowledge workers can discover and share what they know, while simultaneously creating new knowledge. When searching for people, knowledge and expertise, workers reach out to personal networks for a seamless and immediate access to the information, which is tied not just to behavior, but the association between each other in their relationship building. Asking appropriate questions and involving others in the sharing process is crucial. Hearing and sharing an idea, opinion or thought may cause another person to modify his or her thinking into a new, different and escalated fashion.

Social Networking and Collaboration

Since an understanding about knowledge is limited, the uncertainty in American business is in determining a known method of analysis to help managers fully determine who has what intellect and where it is located. This is only a beginning however, as more importantly, gaining access and trust with these people so they are willing to share their knowledge with others they may not have a comfortable relationship must be considered. People are complex and their human capital is the effect of a vast array of stimuli coming from both the internal and external environment. This is because in most cases those in a work environment social network more than likely socialize outside of work also, and as a result a person's human capital may vary and take on different forms with each situation and event. Attempting to control this modification is frightening and quite difficult since the knowledge may be hidden and/or not readily accessible, yet it is imperative that it is managed. A starting location will require first, a change in culture where there is a feeling of safety and trust in all interactions to help reduce any defensive behaviors from sharing. A potential problem is in the methods used in acquiring the information desired, as an example scrutinizing an individual's e-mail, phone records, etc., can be viewed as monitoring, and might contribute to uncomfortable feelings. Secondly, detail a Knowledge Map identifying the central points of contact in order to understand which workers are the most influential within the particular knowledge networks. From here a repository made up of the tacit and explicit knowledge types based on determining their value can be created through the different networks.

There are two types of networking. The first type *formal*, involves official organizational connections, manager to subordinate, through the transmitting of directions and communication regarding business policies, and procedures. Second, is the *informal* personal networks, which are the communities that fill the organizational gaps, providing the relationships, camaraderie, and unknown human capital from others while supplying added magnitude to the information shared. Once the impact that flows through the social networks is recognized and understood, organizations can reduce complexity, redefine roles, service customers and allocate human resources more effectively.

For the organization to gain awareness, managers have to provide personnel opportunities to develop diverse, evolving skills. In doing so, management can help employees interpret past actions, form new attitudes and develop strategies for learning, measuring and evaluating their effectiveness against future efforts. In principle, competition implies that a gain for one is a loss to another, so organizations cannot afford to squander essential resources, often occurring as a consequence of internal competition. The significance of sharing informal knowledge might be in its incompatibility, or possible conflicts introduced by formal structures. Sharing is the center of collaboration. As an effect of informal networks, the impact of collaboration is increased due to the reduced search time and coordination efforts needed to connect to those who have the critical knowledge. Collaboration typically begins by building social relationships through a combined effort. It is crucial that management recognize the existence of informal networks, understand how they might affect the success of any organization, and that their continued self-regulating operation of any method is introduced. By doing so, workers will easily identify the best opportunities to center around. As employees exchange stories they unearth each other's skills, competencies, interests and areas of expertise, which will ultimately foster trust, integrity, respect and support.

Collaboration discouragement is the opposing element for success in a knowledge system. At one time it was common to shy away from fraternization with the competition since they were traditionally regarded as an enemy. Then again, regarding the competition as teachers and partners demonstrating their learning might be more advantageous as it would eliminate any possible aggressiveness. Some argue that sharing know-how brings with it the dissemination of control, but what it actually does is allow knowledge to multiply exponentially. Metcalf's Law and Legacy[5] explains this when it states that the usefulness of a network is equal to the square of the number of users. The product of combining the intellect of two individuals proves to be four times greater than just one. Much the same as the strength arrived at from wind, for example. A 75mph wind is not 3 times the force of a 25mph wind; it is 9 times as strong, the strength of human capital multiplies tenfold when it is leveraged and shared with others involved in similar projects, and furthermore, the knowledge gained from the encounter can be stored for future reference. Distinguishing the human capital unused in ten workers and making it available would provide an organization the exponential knowledge of 100 individuals, making the wealth shared throughout an organization's workforce a major advantage over a competitor. This exponential force is just an indication of how valuable an organization's human capital is and to what extent it can be if made available to be leveraged, shared and harvested. As a rule, knowledge is not captured and stored in a repository, but tacit knowledge can be effective if it is shared and transferred through informal networking. It is the knowledge gained due to socialization and association that is most often extended to helping others lacking in self-gratification.

Evidence shows a large untapped treasure existing with each employee, and that the more socialization, interaction, networking and sharing in the workforce, the more trust, awareness and capability will be developed. Relationships are an investment process that provides a means of dealing with the adversity in our fast changing environment. The more varied the extensive collaborative informal social networks, the easier it becomes for significant knowledge transfers and acquisitions beyond the organization. Organizations cannot possess and create all of the resources possibly required to prosper and grow devoid of collaboration. Although collaboration begins with each individual worker, it is only effective if it focuses both vertically and horizontally throughout the organization.

Although cooperation is essential, collaboration is highly consequential and impressive. Understanding collaboration implies having an awareness of the assimilation of a worker's intellect and its sharing effectiveness with others. A sense of confidence must exist among those who share knowledge and a belief that what is being shared is essential. There are three main reasons for sharing: *repute, reciprocity*, and *altruism*. *Repute* is a factor that encourages people to share since it is believed it will enhance relationship building. When knowledge and/or expertise is shared it is believed they will be recognized as *experts* on various topics and called upon for their awareness; be assigned interesting and challenging assignments; and provided some level of protection in the era of down-sizing and consolidation. Then in conjunction with *reciprocity*, people impart knowledge and/or expertise in the belief that if they share, others will be willing to be a factor to them. Finally, with *altruism*, those who share, do so because they believe it will enhance the overall operation of the organization, which in turn will help them.

The problem surrounding collaboration is that it repeatedly evolves to a situation of *if you scratch my back I will scratch yours*. Companies and the workforce are apt to collaborate in order to get something required in order to do what they do. The exciting aspect of a sharing and collaborative effort is that no one realizes what is taking place and results in a *Win-Win* for everyone. The ideal setting is one where cooperation and collaboration are encouraged and practiced, but the customs are possibly the largest obstacle. To have such an environment, an organization should undergo a significant cultural adjustment, by revolutionizing the alteration of its values, beliefs and mindsets.

As a rule, western cultures are more competitive than collaborative, and if they are to transform successfully, they must focus more on being collaborative. Intrinsically, competition is good, but it forces organizations to compete with those they need to collaborate with to prosper. Where competition can lead to loss, collaboration benefits everyone moving in the same direction. Collaboration is possibly the cornerstone of the Deming philosophy, for the reason that his Win – Win theory of working together for mutual benefit, society at large has greater potential. Deming remembers calling a neighborhood service station for assistance. When the tow truck arrived at his home, he noticed it had the name and address of the service station located on the opposite street corner from the one he had called. When asked why this particular truck had come, the driver explained that neither service station had sufficient business to justify purchasing its own truck, so they collaborated by purchasing one truck to share. Although remaining competitors, the service stations had developed a Win - Win situation.

In contrast, imagine two children each wanting to bake a cake. The children encounter a dilemma when each of their recipes calls for an orange, and only one orange is to be had. After arguing over the one orange and failing to arrive at an agreement neither child is able to complete their cake, resulting in a Lose - Lose outcome. The problem was that the children had not read the recipes thoroughly and had they done so, they would have realized one of the recipes called for the rind of the orange and the other the pulp. From an early age we are taught to compete. In many instances, most find themselves in a Win – Lose situation with the competition, or enemy, standing in the way of success, little realizing the result would be a *Win-Win* for everyone if they collaborated.

Since humans have an innate capacity for collective intelligence, living in a collaborative interactive world enables learning and one where organizations can enhance their benefits by using and re-using its human capital. Practical experience is indispensable, but companies need to realize they will not improve by saying they have a process, improvement only comes when a process is in place. Generally, more valuable learning is the effect of first-hand experience in relationships. Human capital alone cannot be transferred, but can be shared, and in doing so an individual's knowledge can be another person's information. This is especially true when workers collaborate and promote the sharing of idcas.

In today's information age, in an ideal work society, social networking has become the norm and a fundamental economic element given that strength and merit come from variety. To improve efficiency and innovation, it is vital that workers use social networks to access and apply information and knowledge both internally and externally to the organization. The members in an individual's personal social network are people who may collaborate in a variety of distributed areas across the business. When sharing knowledge and/or expertise, people interacting create meaningful, collective thinking and a sense of purpose linking concepts and ideas into common goals. It would be catastrophic to ignore the relationships held by workers. The transition from an autonomous, hierarchical setting to a globally networked one can have profound implications. Failing to use this asset prevents an organization from exploring new relationships and opportunities when trying to surge ahead of its competition.

Value Change

A statement by Andrew Carnegie described it best when he stated: *"The only irreplaceable capital an organization possesses is the knowledge and ability of its people. The productivity of that capital depends on how effectively people share their competence with those who can use it."* Alterations in today's atmosphere have created differences in the method companies are managed. Corporate leaders appear to be playing a game, a high stakes game where the winner is the one who earns the most money. The money is not necessarily for the business leader, but for the scorekeeper who may also be the shareholder. Money appears to have become the measuring stick, and the survival of the fittest has become critical to the relevance of competition. To be number one may lead to winning by any means, often destroying organizational loyalty, honesty, integrity, trust and respect. Winning the game may force personnel to ignore crystal-clear values. Management appears not to understand the importance of the relationship connecting an employee's well-being and organizational endurance, although it has been determined that the values organizations stand for, increasingly affect their ability to function.

Today's managers are measured quarterly on transactions completed, not their quality and to satisfy the outcome sought, some have altered their personal values to arrive at the numbers, which ultimately demonstrates their unethical behavior. Often the numbers are manipulated to fulfill the desired result. At no time in the annals of American business has such a profound shift in managerial behavior been experienced. Never have so many cases of fraud, insider trading and misappropriation of funds been uncovered involving such enterprises as, Enron, Rite Aid, Adelphia, Arthur Anderson, Tyco, Quest, WorldCom and several financial institutions. This is not unique to the U.S. however, as several economic and political scandals have occurred in Europe and the Far East.

Changes have been so profound and have become such an issue that many companies have implemented integrity programs outlining the values employees are expected to follow. These programs are meant to curtail unethical practices, but may be insufficient as they raise doubt as to whether, credible, ethical employees can flourish today. Given that ethics has become such a major aspect of society, future corporate leaders will not only have to concentrate on doing well for the bottom line, but also for society and the workforce. Understanding what energizes employees will help in affecting and sustaining the proper behavior. Reaffirmation of the values-based management system introduced earlier in the 20th century and extended motivation might be a huge step in the right direction.

When an American company experiences problems, the employees are usually the first to feel the effects, usually through cut backs and layoffs. In contrast, the Japanese traditions promote a high emphasis on the labor force by keeping them working, while management assumes responsibility for the business actions. This was recently witnessed with the reduction in auto sales in the U.S. While GM, Ford and Chrysler have let go thousands of employees, ironically with pay due to union contracts, Toyota has kept its employees on the payroll, training them, using them in work teams and having them participate in groups to see how they could improve their processes. The effects have helped Toyota save millions of dollars in improvements and generated new and innovative ideas for when they ramp up to full productivity. If difficult periods continue, overtime is the first thing to be eliminated, and if they still persist senior management is the first to reduce their salaries with the lower levels of management sharing salary cuts if the difficulties continue. This is opposite the manner American companies are operating. In fact, in these times of bailouts one of the questions asked is, "Why isn't management reducing their salaries and forgoing bonuses to help."

Persistent difficulties may lead to teams of workers being formed to perform work that might have gone to outside concerns. The workers are the last to be subjected to any pain. Eventually, if nothing improves, workers are asked to work one day a month without pay. In Japanese corporations, decisions begin at the senior levels with management continually working to determine how to effectively use its employees to overcome restraints and increase growth, which helps to maintain workforce stability. Japanese employees are consulted by management when sales increase and higher production is warranted. Working together, they determine how much, if any additional manpower will be mandatory, if the decision to increase production is made. Consequently, because of their joint decision-making and a feeling of ownership Japanese companies experience the lowest levels of employee mobility.

Value-Chain Relationships

When working to understand interactions between employees and the management system under which they operate, it is important to understand the inherent usefulness of human capital. The term value-chain is usually discussed in reference to system processes and the activities revolving in creating meaning and usefulness for the organization. Understanding these processes requires knowing how human capital is created, integrated, transformed and used from the many relationships within the social networks involved throughout the organization in bringing a final offering to its customers. Value-chain analysis looks at each link in its process chain to determine where meaning is added and how can it be increased, or is a waste, which should be eliminated.

As Nonaka and Takeuchi[6] state *"Organizational knowledge creation should be understood as a process that 'organizationally' amplifies the knowledge created by individuals and crystallizes it as part of the knowledge network of the organization.*"

For human capital to be of significance, strategic assessment is required in dealing with the following aspects:

- What intellectual assets does the organization have or needs to support its strategic objectives?
- What infrastructure will be required to aid with the acquisition, storage and assessment of the human capital, and how will it be controlled for leveraging and sharing?
- Where does the human capital exist, and is it accessible to those who may need it in their work?
- What learning systems should be implemented to encourage replacing the human capital?
- What collaborative dealings and alliances should be established with customers and suppliers as partners, users and providers of strategic knowledge?
- What key actions are required in the human capital process?
- How and where can the human capital be determined

to add meaning?

- How will the effectiveness of the human capital obtained be measured?

There are many different relationships in an organization and it is this networking of individuals in groups that contribute to the value-chain as depicted in Figure 12. The era of the individual contributor is long gone as knowledge creation has become a collaborative effort. Relationships are established and exist as an upshot of common interests and beliefs, and in an organization worker's interests and beliefs may vary. The more sharing of these traits will determine how easily the collaborative sharing of knowledge and/or expertise within the organization is, but it requires a feeling of trust and creditability. Consequently, with relationships being personal, it is essential that any knowledge shared be accurate, applicable and acceptable to those involved.

The universal feeling by all must be one of honesty, trust and openness, all essential in developing, affecting and sustaining relationships. If there is any doubt as to the criticality of the knowledge, inquiry and doubt may make further efforts to share difficult. This will necessitate an agreement of reciprocity where one good turn deserves another.

Value Chain

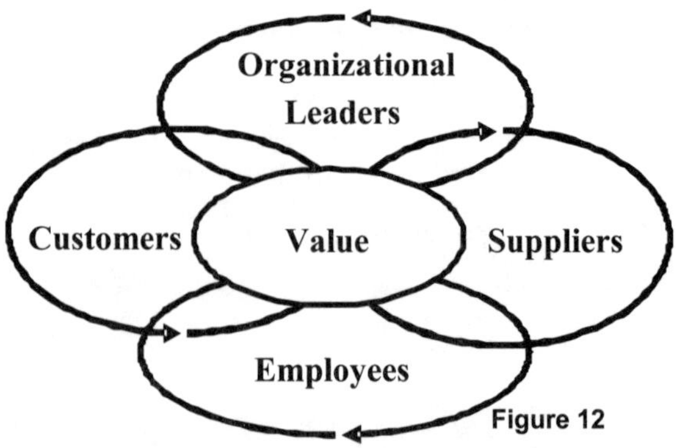

Figure 12

Knowledge Warehousing

There has always been uncertainty about the human brain's capacity to acquire, store and process learning. One school of thought claims the brain has limited capacity, whereas another believes there is no limit to the amount of knowledge the human brain can retain. If one is to believe a limitation exists, then they should believe knowledge is valuable only if it comes from experts. Since learning and human capital development is physical, emotional, intellectual, and comes about on an individual basis, any limitation to capacity is possibly with the organization. Organizational knowledge is similar to the root system of trees in a forest. The brain expands its ability by connecting to new learning encountered much the same as a root system expanding when additional trees are added to the forest. When a tree leaves the system, the loss of its roots creates a void, similar to the loss of human capital when an employee leaves an organization.

Knowledge warehousing is a new concept representing a logical extension of the data warehouse process. Although data warehousing deals with the accessing of relevant information to a few users, it provides an organized, integrated method for the storage and accessing of knowledge. It is possible that developers of the so-called data warehouses are thinking *knowledge* when developing repositories, but in reality, are actually only working with data. Many companies have invested enormous sums for technological systems in order to store and access data for their operating activities, but regardless of size and complexity these systems still lack the ease of storage and access due to inadequate classification methods, and tend to be out-of-date almost immediately. *Knowledge warehousing* should be oriented to an organization's strategic initiatives for operational purposes and IT should provide access to the correct knowledge, to those who require it, when and in the correct format it is required. If stored knowledge can be shared, everybody can benefit owing to the leveraging of the accumulated human capital. The principal problem occurs when accessing the stored knowledge to make use of it in satisfying a new situation or problem.

Most people have become acquainted with the statement, *more is better, bigger is better, and faster is better*, but this statement may not be appropriate when applied to *knowledge warehousing*. The goal is to develop broader, educated problem-solvers who can direct acquired learning to a variety of changing areas. The ability to respond in a suitable, more intelligent and satisfactory manner to customers would be the effect. Utilizing intensified methods of locating, collecting, capturing, structuring, storing and accessing knowledge for leveraging will provide improved quality and flexibility. This will benefit the organization because it allows for magnified prospects of long-term trend prediction and control based on the information and data accessibility.

As a result of capturing, accumulating and storing new learning in a repository, the human capital can be leveraged and shared throughout the organization. Lightning speed access to this asset has become a criterion in enhancing a person's ability to learn and function at a quicker pace. In attempts to bring intellect together it ought to be assumed that it already exists and any additional acquisition will benefit the user. Being able to access value-added learning allows organizations to become more flexible, intense and function more rapidly than the competition at a lower cost.

One of the popular approaches used in recent years to gather and access information and knowledge is through the use of analogues, or obtained cases with a process called *Case-Based Reasoning (CBR)*. CBR is a problem solving method that builds cases by capturing collective knowledge and competencies required to solve similar problems. Whenever a problem is presented, a record of like problems is retrieved and reviewed from the knowledge repository.

The emphasis behind CBR is being able to access managed learning from experiences stored to understand new situations. Current issues are matched against problems captured and later retrieved based on a similarity to the problem defined. Knowledge stored is accessed and re-used in attempting to resolve a similar problem. When a solution is determined, either in matching or determining a new solution, it is then captured, saved and identified as a case in a repository. Some people believe that this method is similar to how human reasoning occurs.

A limitation with the CBR process is that only those who present a problem are referenced, never the ones who may have resolved it originally. Regardless of how advantageous having human capital in a broad-spectrum framework can be, applying a common piece of familiarity to a particular situation may be trying. What is meant for one situation may not be completely applicable in a similar situation, and for this reason regardless of what is available, it is best to use as much exact expertise as possible.

Intellectual Capital Mapping/Mining

Much as the explorers in the Age of Exploration, those who ruled the seas ruled the world. So it is today. Organizations that have mapped, control and analyzed the merit of their human capital control their destiny. Yet, before this is possible, it is required to know where the knowledge, skills, competencies and/or expertise exists, and then publishing a map to publicize where they located, and how to access them in order that an employee can respond and react meaningfully. Developing a knowledge map to determine *what* is needed, *how* it should be processed, *why* it is essential, *where* it can be found and *when* it can or should be applied therefore, becomes imperative. Knowing, and knowing that you know, is the clout behind the force.

In its simplest form a knowledge map is similar to a road

map, used to minimize the time required to arrive at an exact place, while simultaneously providing a direct method for accessing knowledge linked to strategic initiatives. Knowing how this awareness can be applied to understanding the knowledge flows and the method of its access becomes the critical element to those requiring detailed knowledge. Nevertheless, before a knowledge map can be detailed, tools need to be developed to determine the more critical information and then converting it to usable, sharable awareness. This can only be accomplished by understanding the informal structure within the organization to determine where the real sources of competence are located. Identifying the roles of everyone in the structure will help in understanding the effectiveness of the knowledge map.

Some individuals are natural born collectors of knowledge, while others only obtain it as an outcome of any learning, skills and experience. In today's setting, with the decentralization of work efforts and complexity as a product of outsourcing, re-organizing, down-sizing, re-engineering, joint-ventures and multi-organizational project work, it is not easy to know where the knowledge and expertise is, and who has what. In addition, the time required to search for them is reduced and the knowledge infrastructure may break down. Existing awareness is fragmented, difficult to locate and often superfluous and unreliable, but those in need usually know the so-called experts and those more knowledgeable in their local work areas from whom the knowledge required can be acquired. It is central that organizations complete an assessment and develop a map to ascertain and identify the critical and different knowledge types in the core functional areas. Knowledge mapping is the process of identifying the flow meant to help an individual and organization understand where its human capital resides and to prioritize the use of methods and technology for greater effectiveness and efficiency. Of greater importance, the map should reveal implicit knowledge, why it is needed, where it resides, how it can be used to obtain meaning, whether with moderate costs, improved operation or higher productivity. This implies that all knowledge, either newly created, or acquired coming into the organization go through this process.

There are three types of knowledge map structures. The first identifies existing knowledge requirements and gaps in the organization. The second, the informal type, details the so called Social Network, which illustrates how knowledge flows between workers. Lastly, the formal type, analyzes how personnel (and knowledge) are arranged in the work surroundings (sometimes referred to as an Organization Chart). This particular type must also take into account the local customs, culture, social parameters, and changing customer needs and expectations. Getting things accomplished is perhaps only possible by means of informal networks made up of friends or colleagues at work, since it is through the information structures of these networks that knowledge exists.

When searching for organizational knowledge it is essential to center on the normal process of conducting business for the reason that this is where most of the significant discoveries are found. When attempting to uncover human capital, an organization might also stumble onto valuable information that could lead to additional awareness. It is therefore, essential to map and capture the information from all workers, beginning with those planning to leave. Failure to locate and capture essential intellect within the organization implies it may be necessary to go outside to uncover it. Due to wide divisions in organizational hierarchies the problem lies in locating the right people who may have the expertise which is further complicated by diversity, complexity of size, decentralization and telecommuting. One solution would be a map or guide that provides direction to the location of the precise knowledge or expertise.

The effort to gather and capture intellect is not completed until all of the possible human capital in the organization has been captured, archived and structured in a way that it can be accessed. This leads to the question, "What knowledge should be remembered?" The answer will depend on several variables, the particular business, customs and technology involved, problems encountered, judgments made and the rational for each. It is also imperative that the ideas, facts, assumptions, guesses, stories and opinions surrounding the human capital be included. This implies the inclusion of rare, hard to imitate, flexible and durable knowledge from different repositories. Enabling a user to leverage the relevant essential knowledge will require an ability to attain the precise awareness desired quickly. Lastly, to be able to distinguish between what should and should not be maintained is central. This will necessitate that everyone in the organization be included in the process, requiring a conversion, from one of competition to one of collaboration.

Development-Needs Analysis

Human capital cannot be measured unless it is known how it will be used, and to measure it with meaning necessitates knowing and understanding what information is essential for transformational improvement. Measurements are more often quantitative, focusing on cost, competence, time versus qualitative, and centering on human reactions. If it were possible to identify different metrics, additional knowledge and competencies could be interpreted as tangible expectations. This would allow for an easier declaration of measurable values leading to the development of needs awareness. As such, there should be an understanding of the human capital that may require development and corresponding attitudes requiring modification. All of these characteristics make up the workforce's baseline aligned to the organization's strategic initiatives. To determine whether and in particular what development is necessary will call for a *Development-Needs Analysis*. Such an analysis will identify each worker's training and development requirements in determining if there is a lack of appropriate behavior available to perform a task or particular job function; an individual's ability in not satisfying the required performance; and whether it is possible to improve the knowledge and skills to satisfy any skill and competency gaps that might exist.

It is essential that all Development-Needs Analysis are directed to the corporate target. The knowledge and proficiency levels requisite are determined by knowing what specific jobs and tasks are affected and the compulsory human capital entailed as to the importance of the job function. To perform this analysis properly will involve knowing: (1) how often is the task is performed; (2) the amount of time required to complete the task; (3) the type of supervision is required; (4) the degree of difficulty in performing the task; and (5) what skills and competencies are required. Once the assessed information is known it will be possible to determine any required training and provide it to develop the individuals in order to meet the mandatory job working levels. An individual's development has a bearing on his and/or her capability and competency, affecting all dealings in the use of their knowledge. All development will affect the profoundness and breadth of at least one aspect of a person's knowledge. The capability of a person's knowledge varies with the different aspects interacting with one another and functioning alone. Improving only an individual aspect will not ensure improvement of the competency, but will necessitate that the development of knowledge be performed as a synergized whole, and not as a separate element. This is possible if the process begins with an understanding of the organizational efforts and what addressed to satisfy them.

You may be on the right track, but if you stay there long enough, you will get run over.
Will Rogers[1]

Chapter 8

Strategic Knowledge Assessment

With the emergence of the service era, alterations in the 21st century global workplace resemble a whirlwind of turbulence with management searching for ways to drive their organization to a more flexible and agile state. These efforts challenge today's human resources by forcing them into a demanding and time-consuming environment, making new knowledge, skills, competencies and abilities essential. Leaders are constrained repeatedly from responding to business schemes because of inflexible, often inadequate resources, and a workforce with obsolete skills. Given the agenda for growth and responsiveness, combined with the demands for new and better-quality products and services in an agile environment, management has to look internally to its workers to lead the charge. Although organizations usually describe work performed as jobs, other factors are essential when accessing skill levels. The many interactions that may affect an individual's actions, functioning or both should be considered. It is the synergy of the different transactions such as responsibility, drive and individual talent that gives the process meaning. The fewer the number of interactions that can be used in accomplishing a particular task, the better will be the use of the process and one's intellect.

Having an understanding of their values, attitudes and behaviors will insure an enhanced understanding of how workers act and react in interpersonal dealings with others. Some methods are better suited for determining the kinds of information and particular methods workers use in performing their jobs. In determining an individual's competencies, demonstrations and the use of related tasks in performing operations is critical. Workers often have a mix of competencies and their assessment will determine issues such as the: (1) frequency of use; (2) feelings and experiences; (3) availability of patterns of sharing, contribution and levels of operation evidence; (4) nature of the awareness outcomes assessed; (5) expectations of others, and the degree to seeking information as a part of the job; (6) context, situation and sources used; and (7) the organization's strategic initiatives.

The challenge becomes the gathering and examining of the critical few measures and determining the functioning drivers that cause any desired effect or outcome. As stated earlier, the central aim is to satisfy and retain the expertise of the personnel as well as the capturing and sharing of best practices. Although effectiveness measures an organization's ability to achieve desired outcomes, the measurement of outcomes is even more complex when determining organizational effectiveness. The difficulty arises given that effectiveness is based on judgment and execution in *doing the right things* and in *doing them right* to obtain the desired results. According to Drucker[2] the phase, *"doing the right things"* is a standard of efficiency applied to manual work in hopes of reducing costs, but *"doing things right,"* is a standard of effectiveness applied to management efforts. Performing the right things entails performance is aligned with an organization's mission, objectives and purposes, while doing them right implies achieving this desired effort with minimal resources. This validates the importance and needs to analyze what workers do, rather than what it is hoped they do.

To accomplish an assessment effectively will require guidelines for identifying different human capital requirements, but before they can be developed, organizations must know and understand their talent and production resources. One method is by means of a SWOT Matrix (Figure 13); a process that if executed properly will provide direction in identifying, describing, determining and aligning an organization's resources in understanding its strengths (what it can do), weaknesses (can't do) and its opportunities, the things it has potential for doing, and threats, what it will have difficulty in performing. If it is to realize what skills and competencies are required an organization must know their strategic initiatives before attempting a SWOT. From the analysis, differences in the skills and competencies possessed as well as lacking is identified. Once this process has been accomplished an organization will have the information that will help in satisfying its plan, (strengths and opportunities), and the obstacles (weak points and threats), which will have to be overcome or minimized to achieve the desired results. Customarily, with the emphasis on competition a company's limitations are offset by its strengths, and since its human resources and their capabilities represent an organization's strengths, it is crucial that an understanding of both their opportunities and threats are recognized and understood. Completing a SWOT will help in mapping an organization's human capital, illustrating which resources are distinct and unique and how they might support the organization. A proactive scrutiny of an organization's strengths, weaknesses, opportunities and threats is crucial. With this information, an organization is more capable in developing an appropriate plan based on the disparities of current resources with those mandatory in support.

Although there are a variety of tools on hand for conducting performance assessments, it ought to be remembered that techniques dealing with measurements are often vague and or narrowly defined. In either line of attack, two questions must be addressed: (1) are the right things getting measured;

and (2) are the measurements performed correctly? These inquires will require justifying the use of all resources and efforts expended. To do so gainfully, all sources that might contribute to variation in the assessment process should be examined and considered. Understanding the human element involved helps in enhancing an employee's loyalty, which will result in altered behavior. Since organizations are networks of participation, changed behavior will transform an organization. In this new era, learning should be directed to altering behavior because unless it is altered there will be no improvement in performance or productivity.

SWOT

Strengths	**Weaknesses**
Opportunities	**Threats**

Figure 13

Human Capital Assessments and Management

The ideal emphasis in today's emergent atmosphere is to have the proper assessments in place to evaluate individual human capital, then matching them to organizational needs and assigning a value to these resources. Although they admit their intangible assets represent an advantage, many organizations do not know or understand what talent, creativity or potential they have that will give them a competitive advantage. As the focus on assessments and evaluations increases, additional research is vital to determine whether a wider variety of attributes is necessary, and with the advent of service-oriented organizations, intangible assets have come to the forefront.

When intangibles are concerned, in particular their assessment, few standards are available. Assessments are subjective as there is no definite outcome, but if performed properly, the difference linking the desired and actual execution can be determined. No assessment system can present a full and uncomplicated picture of an individual or organization's intangible assets. It is imperative assessments performed in the workplace are performed on an on-going basis using feedback from each person involved. The findings should provide an accurate accounting of a worker's performance in order to make appropriate evaluation. To perform assessments correctly requires going beyond simply collecting data to solve common challenges. It is important that the assessors share responsibility for establishing the defined criteria used in evaluating the performance of an individual's potential in performing a process. When examining attitudes a value judgment is determined from observations and data gathered. As an example, if a low employee absenteeism, turnover and personnel illness are key criteria, and aligned with a conscious or unconscious contribution that will enhance the company's image, it is likely the workforce will have a positive attitude. Conversely, if the reverse is true then the workforce's attitudes are more likely to be negative. Combining competencies based on one's experience, skill level, training, and fairness of policies and procedures will have a major effect on reducing any complication to performing unequivocal functions or tasks. Their interactions can augment complexity and determine the integration of additional functional areas. In the life cycle (Figure 14) three dimensions, Analytical (X axis), Competencies (Y axis), and Value (Z axis) interact. In any assessment effort the measurement dimension must be an aspect of the process that collects and records observations. This effort requires that the directing of objectives to employee behavior and their relationship to results are aligned to an organization's needs and expectations in ways that build worth. To accomplish this effort a needs assessment is required to determine the critical *technological capabilities* relevant to the mission and the efforts required to perform an outstanding job.

The competency dimension occurs when assessed individuals are asked to perform a method used to identify a problem in a particular situation and provide a solution or alternate solution to resolve it. The use of intellect is almost always directed to skills and an individual's capability developed from their use. Skills inter-connected with others reinforcing and strengthening a worker's ability to think, reason and solve problems are known as core competencies. These competencies become value-added if they can produce a customer-perceived meaning, and influence the organization. In order to monitor the skills and realize the effect, organizations are beginning to consider a skills inventory, aligned with a core competency inventory to chart the importance of these skills. Developing one's competencies is not possible purely with education or a training and development program. Because of tacit knowledge, competencies are developed, continually modified, and experienced as is the training used to perform tasks, which will prove to be effective.

As depicted in the life cycle, the z-axis illustrates the value dimension of an assessed individual, which escalates as he or she progresses through life. With this escalation in learning, education, experience and development vital to satisfying their targets, organizations are able to determine a realistic monetary resolve for their personnel. From this outcome a legitimate and realistic ROI can be resolved.

LIFE-CYCLE

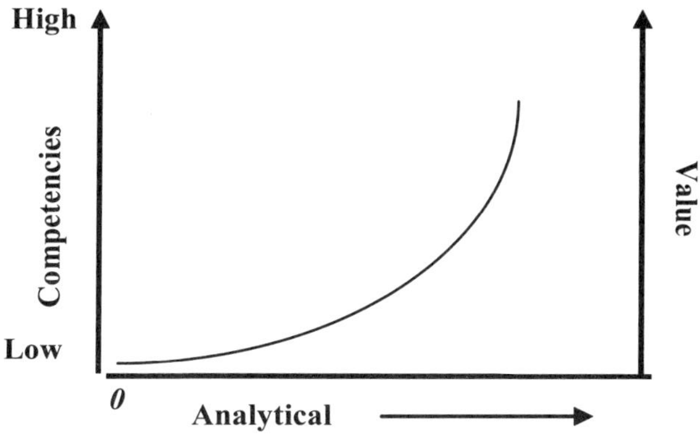

Figure 14

The human capital assessment process must become a *life-style,* where the workforce is agreeable to having their knowledge and competencies assessed on-going and willing to participate and discuss their feelings. This requires a sense of compassion and belief, something only possible if every person has deference for one another's knowledge, understands the disparity, is confident that what is identified will not be used for adverse purposes, and the process will make a difference. To address the transformation, a coordinated line of attack designed and implemented across all distributed sources will be required to ensure that all training and development activities include a common core of learning. New training courses in evaluation methods and usage will be compulsory for all managers. Every person must have a clear understanding of what is expected of the assessment process. This expectation will necessitate that all personnel in each functioning area have clear operation standards, which are reinforced and then applied to individual contributions on top of management. A norm promoted to evaluate actions, skills and competencies, where an on-going execution is chief, as well as peer review techniques with performance standards identified. No assessment process can address all facets of training or learning effectiveness, but with planning and design, a number of useful criteria can help in determining justification for training and education.

Assessing one's knowledge is complicated. Employees need to be assessed when creating, performing or demonstrating their competencies in real-life situations. Any assessment should reflect what is known and directed to the application of practical problems while utilizing a variety of strategies. The problem may not be in determining what knowledge each individual lacks, but in what is required. To determine whether a development need is necessary will require assessing the shortfall of the action experienced.

Although key to knowing how to perform, it is critical to know *when* to perform and then *how* to bring the performance needed into play. When implementing an assessment process the problem is not with obtaining information, but with its ethical use. One possible method to overcome this is with employee self-assessments, where their particular proficiency and abilities is declared. Another method might be with the administering of tests and checklists developed for assessing each employee's human capital. Lacking a method of substantiation as to applying the knowledge, is only hear-say. Still another technique would be to judge with observable criteria the employee's execution and work output with defined standards, insuring advanced communications and fewer misinterpretations of the effects. There are other potential problems that can be aligned to the intangibles associated with evaluating each individual contributor's knowledge. Since assessing inferred knowledge can only be done through subjective observation and judgment, it is difficult to establish standards. To assure exactness, validity and dependability it is vital that the observable criteria be;

(1) defined and specifically established (best satisfied using *action* verbs); (2) aligned as close as possible to expected outcomes; (3) examined in a relationship of *Why* versus *How* processes are performed; and (4) observed in a central self-developing interest by the workers for continual development and gaining of new skills beyond their jobs. It is central for any assessment process to be correlated to the instruments used in assessing the organization's strategic initiatives, and those used to represent the primary aspects of the criteria that determine human capital.

People do not favor being assessed, and an individual's perception can distort the outcome since each may have a different perspective to looking at things. Perception of different types of viewpoints brought into any process will have varied levels of importance. Regardless of the business, demographics, or community, a worker is a part of a diversified group. The more workers mix with others the more likely they are to profit from the contributions, strengths and insights brought by others. Although the inconsistency of the methods used in an assessment is a hindrance, even more difficult are the difficulties that correspond to determining a technique appropriate for assessing intangibles. To help in eliminating these problems it is best if the assessed employees are members of a support group, which should include peers, team members, managers, supervisors, customers, suppliers and any others involved.

Measurement as a Tool in Decision-Making

One reason methods for measuring competencies have been slow in developing is a level of credibility with consistent approaches for assessment. Since individual performance is often subject to subjective characteristics that may not be observed, it is difficult to completely assess employees. Consequently, it is critical that new goal-oriented and actionable objective measures are developed.

If applied correctly, measurements are invaluable and can provide information about an organization's developmental and resource requirements needed to stay competitive. To be meaningful the measurements must be reliable, repeatable, valid, and linked directly to the organization's initiatives. Unfortunately with measurements comes uncertainty. Are the right things getting measured? Is *what* is known measured? Are the process owners also doing the measuring? Is management aware of how the human capital available will benefit the measured organization? The few tools to be had lack the aptitude basic to predicting the future skills considered central for introducing new opportunities. Accordingly, current methods are unable to collaborate across distributed sources to capture the intra-organizational dynamics occurring in the workplace with customers and suppliers that might help with predicting what action the marketplace could take. To do so requires that human capital be understood and structured in order that an organization can focus on what is desirable to remain competitive. In this manner, management is able to address the internal and external setting of the business and address whatever is necessary to deal with the changing demands.

In view of the fact that implicit knowledge is difficult to measure, assessment programs seldom gauge an individual's progress. Foreign to most management, this is an area not well managed. Based on a survey by Information Systems Research (ISR)[3], few executives measure their human capital, even though they concur that these means escalate in usefulness the more they are engaged.

The effect of any actions occurring in any assessment process is made up of three phases. The first, the *Preparation* phase, requires strength on the part of the assessors, who must be compassionate, unbiased and continually working to solicit the data and information decisive in making the assessment process successful. In addition, having the ability to assess workers in difficult situations is central. This is because whenever the human element is involved, emotions, attitudes, individual beliefs and feelings must be addressed along with the constant interference occurring in the assessed person's thought process. No less important is the need to understand the organization's strategic initiatives in order to suggest the right scope of the assessment and to provide suggestions after the process is complete.

Execution, the second phase, is where the actual assessment occurs directed to what the workers are doing and the evaluation of their performance. This phase requires that defined tasks be performed in order to determine the outcomes and the effectiveness of what occurs corresponding to *how well* the results are projected. These particular actions require that the pre-determined assessment instruments used in the process are referenced to maintain reliability. In the last phase *Reporting*, the outcomes are reported once the findings are accumulated and evaluated. Here the results are shared with all interested persons and groups, especially those assessed. Consequently, all workers will develop an understanding of the assessment process and benefit from the outcome.

New and different methods are vital in determining the information critical to verify conduct in the workplace. The outcome of any assessment in the work setting should provide, *who has what*, *who* requires what, and *how much* further development is considered necessary in particular areas. It is crucial that all employees be involved in determining the process ability and efficiency levels revolving around *how much*. It is agreed that most workers have the potential to do extra, but for varied reasons do not function to their fullest capability. Job descriptions given to employees are usually nebulous, not descriptive and seldom applicable to the current requirements. The reason for this may be because management has never defined its initiatives or identified a vision and mission. Requirements therefore are unclear at best, and by not understanding what human capital is crucial it is impossible to determine what and to the extent it exists in the workplace.

Since acquired knowledge is often fixed to a particular area it is imperative that each significant aspect is examined, and include a clear-cut conventional description to provide a common understanding of each aspect's meaning. Yet this may create some concern. A worker's functioning is commonly determined simply by observation, which is an inadequate method for evaluating employees, especially across functions. To gauge a worker's exertion accurately cannot be visually performed easily, let alone compared to another, since it is a matter of data compiled over-time that is needed for evaluation. An accurate assessment can only be made of each person's effort and proficiency level by assessing the meaningful aspect, and accumulating the proper data, which will allow for determining a monetary worth. Only with this method will it be possible to determine how effective intellectual resources can be employed in the future from an economic standpoint. When assessing an individual's human capital, the usefulness to be determined should include their ability to transfer human capital to the job. This effort needs to include harnessing an individual's human capital in different functional disciplines such as testing, design, and project management abilities. Valid and reliable methods of assessing acquired human capital may include interviewing, a technique used to probe what an individual has said or how they performed when involved with a specific task. During this process, participants outline what is needed to know to perform particular jobs, and this knowledge is used to help others understand so they can replicate the methods used should they do they work. In addition, think aloud protocols and the collecting of information about an individual's problem-solving methods and ways of collecting evidence of attained learning through recorded sessions and reviews should be employed. These are processes that monitor an individual performing a work function, then reviewed with them by means of a third party, who can help by compiling additional information about what was performed.

No two individuals have the same competencies, making it even more essential that an organization's human capital be categorized. The Knowledge Measurement Profile (Figure 15) illustrates the interactions between Soft-Skills and Technical Competencies. In unison, the competencies influence the significant skills and/or those possessed by an organization. The *Soft Skills,* appearing on the X-Axis, identify *how* an employee might function. In this grouping the assessor's efficiency elements such as motivation and a willingness to perform the assessment significant for the 21st century work milieu should be included. The Y-axis identifies the *technical competencies*, which detail *what* can be done. These competencies enable the successful execution of a process, allowing workers the ability to *work smarter*, for the reason that they are able to implement and make use of their and other worker's human capital in the workplace. Understanding *what* to do when something is to be performed is imperative and a pre-condition for knowing *how* to accomplish a particular task, but it is insufficient. Of more importance are the issues of difficulty, a willingness to act and responsiveness to perform a particular task.

In examining the Knowledge Management Profile, four patterns unfold from the two continuums into which workers are force-ranked. In our analysis we see where the *Incomplete,* the first quadrant (LL), represents inferior capability due to deficiencies in both Soft-Skills and Technical Competencies. Individuals categorized in this quadrant would be found to be lacking in the types of competencies identified as significant for today's workplace. Those in this quadrant might be semi or unskilled and would most likely be labeled as poor performers with a low efficiency capability who should be replaced. In contrast, individuals categorized into either of the two *Partial* quadrants (LH or HL), would have either a high-level of *soft-skills* combined with a lack of *technical competencies*, or a lack of *soft-skills* combined with a high-level of *technical competencies*. Although the workers in these quadrants would be productive, their output might be late in coming and below standard, but with some development they could undergo some improvement. Those categorized in either of these quadrants might have means that would prove to be valuable and effective in particular situations to the organization, and it will be management's responsibility to determine what characteristic deficiency the employee might have that is acceptable. In some situations *technical skills* are the dominant characteristic required, while leadership qualities are less important, or just the opposite. Management has the responsibility to decide what the important criteria is, and how significant are the skills and competencies for the situation confronted.

Knowledge Measurement Profile

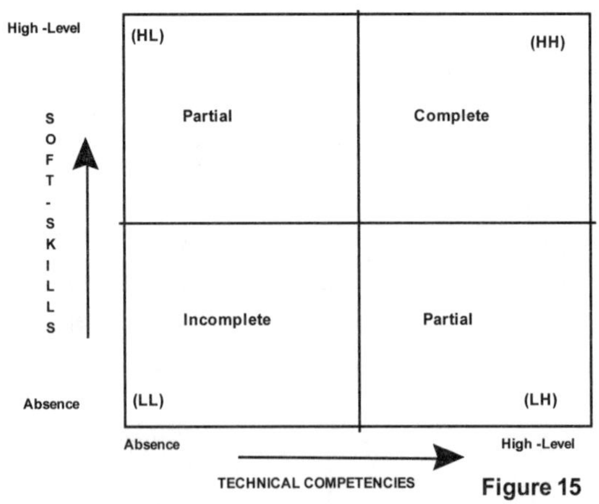

Figure 15

Individuals categorized into the *Complete* quadrant (HH) demonstrate a high-level presence of both *soft-skills* and *technical competencies*. The *Complete* quadrant is the supposed ideal, and individuals categorized in this quadrant may have competencies that may also be scarce. This quadrant usually contains persons who are believed to have a more positive attitude and are more productive and motivated. Identified as leaders, they are apt to be believed irreplaceable in their roles. Regardless of the quadrant employees are force-ranked into, their skills and competencies should be regarded and consistent with all job requirements. Simply maintaining the *best and the brightest* may not be the ideal business decision because even if the employees may have the relevant job skills, the attitudes, values and cultural fit indicative of superior work may be lacking.

When he was the CEO of General Electric, Jack Welch believed that in preparing the company for the 21st century only recruits who fall into the *Complete* Quadrant (HH) should be recruited. Consequently, all GE personnel are force-ranked into categories of varying competencies and knowledge referred to as A, B and C players. Without a doubt, if the workers were asked, almost all would state they were *A* players who should be categorized into the *Complete* Quadrant (HH). Welch was not the first to differentiate human resources in this manner, as in its maturing years in the 80's Apple used this characterization to attract and retain a superior caliber of employee. This has led to companies such as Ford, Cisco Systems, ConocoPhilips and Sun Microsystems adopting this categorization process.

The *A, B and C* players were later categorized into three 20 – 70 – 10 %ages. In theory, this idea might work, but in reality it fails. The idea behind the %ages is to classify the top 20% of the workers as *A* players, identified as the cream of the crop, the next 70% *B* players are believed to be able to be further developed as required, and the remaining 10%,

C players should be encouraged to leave as no funds will be spent on developing them. Eliminating the bottom 10% of the workers implies that the LL category (C players) would have to be made up of 10% of the employees who had been force-ranked earlier into the two higher quadrants. This process sounds good, but in reality the A players are in demand and they can readily leave for broader positions and more money to other companies. This will leave the B players: the capable steady performers who make up the majority of the workforce with no mentors or a support group. Eventually the force-ranking process will continue until the last remaining employee in the company would be an *A* player and he or she could turn off the lights on her way out. Another fault with this process is that all new employees are rated in the *A* category for their first year, and because of the need to satisfy the %ages others are often forced into categories they might not have been classified into otherwise. In addition, since the categorizations are based on subjective data employees may also be categorized improperly as an effect of invalid opinions and judgments. It doesn't end there however. Managers at each level of the organizational structure are assigned %ages and consequently, employees are sometimes reclassified repeatedly to a lower level to meet the %age before the force-ranking process is complete. Ultimately, employees are classified by managers who may not know or have even seen them and some are simply ranked given that they are in a similar salary range. Additionally, there is little consideration as to the length of time the employees may have been with the company or their responsibilities. These particulars illustrate the inadequacies in assessing those who may come from different functional areas and force-ranking them with others who may have more competence, awareness and education. There have been some repercussions from this process as lawsuits have been brought against employers such as Ford, Mansanto and others because of discriminatory assessments made, resulting in many early adopters of this process eliminating its use.

Robert Reich[4] in discussing human capital shared some disturbing information with his statement, "If we do not make this property more widely available, if we do not invest in the intelligence of all our citizens, we shall have a divided society." The division of society may already exist, and growing at a phenomenal rate. Reich divided the workforce into categories as shown in Figure 16 that can be correlated to the Technical and Soft-skills interactions depicted in Figure 14. His first group, the *Routine Operators,* can be aligned to the (LL) *Undesirable* quadrant in the preceding matrix. Reich identified this group as service providers who make up approximately 25% of the workers. The work performed by this group is often the first to be automated, eliminated or directed to off-shore countries where the labor costs are cheaper. This particular quadrant might include the workers in the few remaining United States manufacturing jobs, and those who may have a problem communicating in English. The next 30%, Reich's second group, is known as the *Personal Service Providers*. The workers in this group provide a special service such as security and health care in a hospital, and fall into either the (HL) or the (LH) *Questionable* quadrants depicted. The last group is referred to as the *Symbolic Analysts* by Reich, made up of the so-called experts; the knowledge workers; attorneys, doctors, educators and financial experts, in essence the professionals. It is this 20% of the workforce that Reich believes have the might and influence in our society. In examining the groups further, Reich sees a greater division of our society in after-tax income. The *Symbolic Analysts* have a greater after-tax income than the other two groups combined; the 80 – 20 rule. Reich believes it is the children of this group who usually go on to complete higher education, while many children of the other two groups either drop out at a young age or seldom complete an upper-level degree. This deficiency in education is felt in the workplace and the community today; evident with the reduction in the numbers of new products and services, poorer quality and less customer satisfaction encountered in the marketplace. Farmers, miners and government workers make up the remaining workforce. Routine work may require few soft-skills or competencies, and little value-added work, yet it is required work. Should plans be put in place to get rid of those categorized in the *undesirable* quadrant, management must determine how their work will be performed or how it can be satisfied in a different manner. The adage, "if you automate a poor process; you end up with an automated poor process," should be considered.

Workforce Divisions

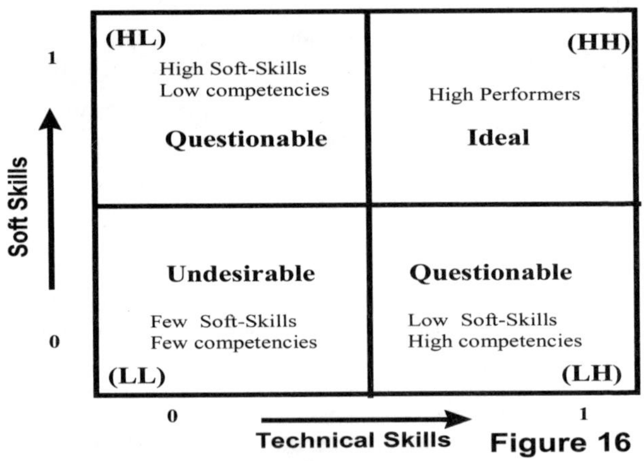

Figure 16

Assessments and Evaluations

To assess requires an understanding of how to determine what an individual knows and is able to do. Evaluations in turn are somewhat different, in that they do not just help in improving performance and productivity, but can facilitate in increasing an employee's capabilities. Assessments in turn are used to organize information in determining what human capital exists, is useable, being worked on and the method by which it will be used. Evaluations determine the financial significance the knowledge might provide and how it might best satisfy the organization's objectives. Assessments of various kinds have become a tool in an attempt to expand the understanding of the needs of developing organizations while providing an accurate estimate of an employee's functioning, attitudinal concepts and managerial abilities.

In defining assessment as it relates to human capital it could read as *a method used to determine the knowledge possessed by an employee.* In so doing, it must be realized that each individual's intellect is different and constantly changing. Assessments are meant to apply quality metrics that will ultimately help in generating improved performance and greater productivity, but what is intended and necessary must also be measured.

Any assessment process requires a significant liability by management as the effort requires continual monitoring and a sustained evaluation of each employee's development. The assessment process should begin with an understanding of what human capital is crucial to satisfy the organization's strategic objectives, and then identifying the explicit knowledge and skill sets that exist. Lastly, the process must allow for the building of an human capital repository for the captured information and to determine ways to leverage and share what is distributed across the organization. The complete process for conducting the assessment will be a learning occurrence, with an emphasis to turn tacit knowledge into explicit knowledge. The products of the described process should influence and assist in planning future training for employee development and help link new to acquired learning and experiences. Once determined, it will be easier for management to define relevance for any developments processed.

There are three formats by which the manual, interactive

and automated methods of assessing knowledge can be performed. The first is a *structured* format related to specific work tasks aligned to objectives, where the results could be used as measures of business practices. In the second, the *semi-structured* format, knowledge is determined from a script. Lastly, the *unstructured* format consists of several methods of knowledge acquisition such as walking around the workplace making notes of observations and communicating by asking generic questions. This process requires that the assessors have cognition of the theories of non-verbal communications, kinesics (body language) and polemics (the art of dispute or argument). The unstructured format is valuable given that communications requires more than just time-honored verbal and listening skills. It involves an ability to read and interpret body language. By adopting non-verbal patterns, a person can help others to relax, be more responsive and have greater empathy. Understanding methods of communications is not sufficient unaided. Through this means one has the ability of having a significant influence on relationships, especially the need to promote a feeling of devotion, loyalty, sincerity and openness with others. An assessor needs an understanding of people's behavior and for knowledge of the theory of motivation. Understanding what motivates an individual's efforts, what hinders them and knowing how to overcome fear/avoidance reactions is crucial.

Communication skills are the foundation of social life, and the totality of behaviors involving the sharing of information. Together these elements assist in managing the investment in the human capital and new technological capabilities available. People understand the importance of listening, but few expend the resources and energy to help them learn proper listening skills. Listening is different to hearing, and lacking the ability to listen, truly listen, hearing is not possible. A common problem that occurs is when people seemingly tune out something they do not wish to hear, and ignore information believed not relevant or in concert with perceived ideas. While listening can lead to additional data, not hearing makes it impossible to develop an in-depth understanding of what is shared. Learning is only accomplished when deemed worthwhile and aligned to something already known, and when shared it has a significant impact on what is already known by the receivers. For intellect to be far-reaching and effective, an understanding of experience, trust and the contextual experiences of the sender and receiver involved in this sharing process is essential. The criterion for acceptance is whether or not the sender has developed credibility and a willingness to share. People learn best by means of informal contextual learning relating to real world situations and their application. Utilizing online video-conferencing technology is one method that helps people learn from one another, and one that has allowed the conducting of awareness exchange sessions as a type of informal virtual water cooler social network. Owing to this process a large amount of the work performed is accomplished because workers are constantly communicating with one another, learning through the capturing and sharing of knowledge, experiences and insights. In addition to these informal social networks, organizations must determine new and different methods to organize and accumulate knowledge into a central repository that can be accessed as required allowing the workers the ability to continually learn in support of decision-making and problem-solving efforts.

To make communications effective in the human capital venue attention is important and must be directed to the understanding and feedback processes. A possible instrument to help in this conclusion may be the following *Knowledge Equation* whose attributes contribute to each individual's human capital repository and effectiveness.

K (Intellectual Capital) = f (L, S, E, A, B)
Where L = Learning (Gen'l Knowledge)
S = Skills (Capabilities)
E = Experience
A = Attitude (Mind-sets)
B = Behavior (Job related)

Effective human capital can be determined by addressing all of the different elements of the *Knowledge Equation* and knowing how well they are aligned with an organization's needs. In assessing the elements used in the equation, it is critical to determine particular attributes. This probe is meant to determine each individual's ability in different skills, range of experience, attitude (i.e. motivation level, interest in expanding knowledge) and behavior in the workplace. Central to the equation, is an understanding of the strengths, weaknesses and development needs of each individual across the organization. When in the company of young children, people are often reminded of their grown-up reluctance to bring a child's attitude to work. A child's inquisitiveness and questioning process of always asking *Why,* in their development, is an excellent lesson. If adults acted in a similar manner they might learn a great deal more.

In determining intellect levels it is imperative to consider the following assessment principles: The first, *Purpose,* allows for satisfying the *Why* and *What* of assessments. It is most important that the process is not regarded as a performance appraisal, but one of information gathering and the assessed person understanding *what they need to know* in addition to the process, given that the assessment cannot be performed in isolation.

Creating a relaxed atmosphere will help the assessed individual function at the highest possible level. *Responsibility,* the second principle, deals with the *Who* is involved in the entire process. Each individual should be regarded as a full partner who accepts accountability for the effects and develops an understanding of *who needs to know* for improved planning of future development. The third principle, *Involvement,* directs attention to the *How* things are done in the process. This principle provides qualitative information that will help in evaluating *how the knowledge* can be shared in helping with future investments in people, planning, and guidance. The last principle, *Feedback*, provides a tracking method for the continual development and processing affect that will assist in distinguishing between poor articulation and the lack of awareness.

Performance assessments are often based on past data and conditions making it difficult to determine future expectations. No firm decisions for the future can be made as an upshot of such assessments as insights gained are relative. Looking at the system, a group of interdependent conditions can make the assessment more valuable with appropriate conclusions. The tools and materials used for an assessment, in addition to the assessors, process, and in particular the locale where it takes place are just a few of the varying elements that make up the system. More importantly, the tools will also assist in helping each individual focus on his or her forte, helping them to excel in the things they do well and not on those they don't. Some methods (tools) that could be of assistance are: (1) *360-Degree evaluations*: a method by which those in the realm of influence describe how the individual is perceived; (2) *Checklist evaluations* of live or recorded performance. Trained evaluators check off the actions, behaviors, activities or both, observed against a checklist; (3) *Record reviews*: reviews of an employee's work history, their training and development accomplishments; (4*) Oral tests* by which an individual being evaluated is asked a range of questions on his or her ability in accumulating and reasoning skills; (5) *Written exams*: used to determine an individual's comprehension and understanding of a defined body of knowledge; (6) *Surveys* used to assess the quality of a person's intellect and attitudes about particular tasks, functions or both; (7) *Simulations and Models*: methods which allow for the measuring of complex tasks or functions; (8) *Portfolios:* repositories of an individual's work account samples, which can be evaluated based on pre-determined criteria in assessing competencies and determining knowledge; (9) *Live or recorded performance:* where evaluators observe real life execution; (10) *Productivity levels:* methods using customer assessments to determine a standard of operation; and (11) *Documentation of behaviors:* containing the evaluation of an individual's behaviors as aligned to professionalism, work habits, values and habits of life-long learning.

When given development assignments individuals depend on their habits, and as a result may apply incorrect or outdated knowledge to new situations. Customary methods may no longer be valid and management must realize that the desired effects in the form of ideas, interactions, processes and technical advances may not always be the explicit knowledge it was in the Industrial Age. Today's position is not about amassing intellectual assets; it is about obtaining usefulness from what is available. This implies the intellect of each employee be assessed for relevance to the organization and completeness for context, breadth and depth. It is important that data accrued via the different assessment methods is relevant in order that decisions made will help achieve the desired outcome. Consequently, it will be possible to help workers attain new knowledge, develop new skills, competencies, and working relationships.

Self-improvement and self-assessment are critical in an individual's quest to improve their job corresponding execution. People require the ability to think critically in order to determine what criteria should be used to judge and apply objectivity to their work. The art of questioning needs to be cultivated like a key that opens the door to improvement. Regardless of the type of improvement sought, probing will provide the answers by identifying the patterns, bad habits and mistakes made and provide meaning to the organization. Questions help in determining methods to reduce costs, improve cycle time, increase yield and introduce new ways to drive change and adapt to a person's work. The following inquiries can help in providing the success expected in business and in life:

- Why is this process performed here?
- Why is it done this way?
- Why is it performed at this time?
- How can I perform my job better?
- How can defects be reduced?
- Is there another method that can be used to perform this task?
- Is there someone who knows more about this?

Seeking out answers will satisfy the questions, which can help in changing the methods used in the work place. Of course, asking questions is only possible in a setting of open communications. It is vital that assessment processes foster additional learning as an aspect of their work area, but a potential obstacle is the transforming of perceptions into assumptions and bias about the aspects in the process being assessed. Reasons why the process requires planning and monitoring are; (1) the continual improvement of the process; (2) insuring the procurement of assets that will or can be leveraged; and (3) having an awareness of the knowledge required to satisfy the objectives.

It is not possible to employ reasonable, precise and

predictive models of intangible assets possessed by others. Currently no known measure whether general, useful or objective enough for making subjective judgments can be found. What is crucial is a generic framework for accumulating, cataloguing, managing and leveraging knowledge. This necessitates the realization of: how and what criteria can be used in assigning meaning to the different knowledge elements; what theoretical leverage exists to improve the organization's ability in identifying its human capital; and when and how statements about human capital are confirmed?

Profound Measurement Approaches

The most common reason for any human capital measurement is to determine whether the business actions and outcomes are able to be satisfied with the skills and competencies presented and what learning might be required to fill any gaps. This implies that assessments of one's ability in performing a task correctly, effectively with consistency, under varying conditions and performed to a high quality are vital. To do so effectively will require deliberate approaches to measure and assess because what gets measured gets done. The targets intended for any defined measurements need identification and effects dealt with strategically, and directed to behavioral modification. Measurement issues such as superior work, greater motivation, pride, self-confidence, satisfaction of one's achievements and altered attitudes will require that management have new tools. Using rating scales or checklists as assessment instruments will require proficiency levels evaluated, whether or not functions are performed, whereas anecdotal records might help in assessing an individual's attitudes. Any measurement tactic should emphasize an eventual goal for determining a particular attribute contributing to some form of evaluation to expand critical requirements. This assessment process requires knowing what attitudes are expected on top of the different experiences important in order for the assessed personnel to reveal their level of competency. Dependable metrics should be expressed as a numeric value for each of the different areas identified, in order to make proper decisions.

Kirkpatrick[5] identifies four levels of performance measurements. The first, *Reaction*, corresponds to a learner's satisfaction from a learning experience, and is often determined by having the learner complete an evaluation survey after any training to compile information as to the training's validity and relevance. *Learning*, the second level, deals with how well the learner has comprehended the material taught, using pre and post-tests to determine whether the learning obtained was that intended. The third level, *Behavior*, interacts with the learner's ability to leverage new learning in the workplace into effective behaviors. Although mostly subjective, in this level, observations, additional responsibilities and continual reviews by managers, peers, customers, suppliers and self-assessment methods are used to determine the learning obtained and changes in behavior. Lastly, *Results*, the fourth level, is a self-assessment process meant to determine the effect of learning as it is aligned to the employee's work. This process must be proactive in order that the different abilities and key competencies are valued properly. It is from the information compiled using a multiple of the above-mentioned methods that greater meaning and help in lessening controversy and issues of eligibility will be achieved.

This writing proposes a proactive process of self-assessment to determine an employee's intellect level entering into the measurement process and continuing throughout their development. I believe the process actually introduces a new level, one that precedes Kirkpatrick's first level that might be referred to as the *Introduction* level. Regardless of Kirkpatrick's simplistic method, assessment is not a straight forward linkage between the assessed individual and the instrument used in the process. With this introductory level it will be possible to determine an individual's intellect, expertise, skill level and competencies acquired earlier to any new training and development. This new level may also be the missing element in the transfer of learning.

Measurements are an attempt to formulate concepts useful in influencing a worker's performance and behavior. This information will help in identifying the interactions changing or influencing the inferred knowledge usefulness to the organization. What is measured will communicate what is critical when the assignment of a numeric value is determined under constant and varying conditions. The unfortunate aspect of measuring is the fact that usually only the easiest things get measured. Understanding and quantifying all possible measurement errors is an aspect often overlooked when assessing knowledge, but decisive in determining an effective method by which business resources are or will be used. It is also essential to include the measurement system, which ought to include measures sensitive enough to insure credibility. Measurements are critical if organizations are to learn from their practices and benefit from the leveraging of their knowledge. New and creative methods for measuring and complimenting one's functioning as an outcome of change are vital. Demonstration of a skill is one of the heightened methods for determining an individual's competencies and capabilities, as it provides factual evidence. Workers would prefer having an opportunity to share competencies for improving workplace efficiency than to be measured incorrectly. It is essential therefore, that all measures of execution and intellect are appropriately and thoroughly assessed. By adhering to the truism *you cannot manage it, if you do not measure it,* management can move into the future with the correct information understanding of how human capital can add credibility. To arrive at this level will require that management formulate a strategic tactic to placing significance to the human capital making it possible to determine the company's worth, thereby enhancing shareholder value. Many organizations grapple with the growing interest of measuring human capital because it involves the human element, something central to determining merit, but often ignored and/or overlooked. It would be admirable if all organizations were measuring their human capital given that business worth is determined when the focus is on its core competencies, yet in many situations this is not the situation. The growing number of mergers in today's venue involves companies with different focuses, purposes and directions, each creating unknown problems in determining human capital merit. Lacking an understanding of their human capital, the hopes of an organization experiencing desired value-added behavior and validating unexploited opportunities in the workforce are near impossible.

Although new tools and methodologies are being introduced at an accelerated pace, management still has difficulties with determining the proper relevance of human capital for further creation, utilization and dissemination. An example is seen with the so-called *Blue Collar* workers; the front line personnel who may not have abundant informal education, but who have a depth of implicit knowledge developed over years of work experience. Unfortunately, their awareness is seldom monitored with measures defined in procedures and as an upshot they may often be interpreted as poor performers. Metrics are important if used correctly and relate to how well the system is functioning. Using qualitative measures such as *a little*, *a lot*, or *not enough* are used habitually, and devoid of a proper metrics focus on precise quantitative measures utilizing operational definitions, efforts might possibly be directed incorrectly.

Operational Skill Level Dimensions

Research suggests that approximately 700 implicit and explicit human skills can be recognized. Although some are perhaps more adept in different skills than others, it is difficult for an individual to master more than six or seven. Whereas certain skills or combinations of such may produce greater results, others are no less useable, but may encourage the use and development of others leading to an added ability with lesser-used skills. Therefore, these skills can be used with ease resulting in a more diverse employee. The central aspects of the process is in knowing what knowledge, skills proficiencies and behaviors are required, and have the ability for improving less proficient skills identified.

There are two types of skills. *Evaluator skills,* the first type, is used to access the capabilities required, while the second type, *conductor skills,* perform the activity critical to using the capabilities identified. As an example, an *evaluator skill* might be the ability to demonstrate key business realization and measurements (market, products/services, competition, performance measures, etc.). This knowledge would come as a consequence of having a *Business Acumen* competency, while the ability to use the Excel software, an associated *conductor* skill to develop a spreadsheet would come from the Information Technology's Expert competency. Following are some examples of Personal Attributes, Core Competencies, and associated skills:

Examples might be as follows:

Competencies	Measurable Actions
Technology	Understands the intent and can develop procedures, identifies tools, understands proper resources or both crucial to solving problems.

Skills	Measurable Actions
Communications	Conveys ideas and information clearly and openly.
Creativity	Identifies best practice approaches to performing work functions which result in time savings, quality of work, and value.
Delegation	Distributes workload and responsibility evenly.
Motivation	Can create enthusiasm, excitement, and commitment within the parties involved producing improved and quicker results.
Team Building	Works well with team members in an environment of cooperation, collaboration, sharing, skills and knowledge abilities.
Performance	Tasks are executed with a sense of urgency and a drive to win. Makes a difference on to all tasks and develops a reputation for delivering results.
Job Knowledge	Has a strong functional competence and is proficient in a business/technical discipline, and is always looking to employ this expertise in other areas of the business.
Education	Continually works to expand his/her education by expanding and developing an educational background such as learning finance and different cultures. Develops training as well as functional skills.

Group Interaction	Studies psychology, learns about group dynamics, is involved with people in different work environments, multi-functional teams, process initiatives, etc.

Assessing Competencies

Companies must continually assess their human resources and abilities to determine what competencies require updating. This information is critical to addressing main challenges in the 21st century workplace. With no correct understanding of the competencies it has, or their availability, an organization is doomed to failure. Competencies highlighting the skills, capabilities and technologies important for a strategic advantage, are the motivating force for the success of an organization. It is difficult to separate competencies as they are often developed through learning-by-doing. This is a process by which workers learn how to coordinate skills and integrate them with diverse resources, operations and technologies. The end result of this process is the ability to apply this learning into observable actions. Some believe individuals should concentrate on using and improving their strengths. Exerting too much effort to their shortcomings; or the competencies lacking or deficient in can prevent an organization from developing a sustainable advantage.

The American educational system misuses most of its time and money addressing an individual's deficiencies rather than their strengths. As a result, people are not encouraged to appreciate their strengths. Alan Weise[6] states that business efforts appear to be designed and directed in much the same manner as a baseball trainer trying to raise a baseball player's .220 Runs Batted In (RBI) average to .230 instead of directing the same efforts toward raising a player's .315 RBI average to .320, which would generate greater results. If a worker's intellect were further managed, his/her employability could be contracted with greater effectiveness, higher efficiency, enhancement and productivity; opening the possibility for new business opportunities. The strengths developed are founded by a worker's attitude toward cooperation, collaboration and sharing, but forms of strength that may also be a shortcoming must be realized. Workers recognized as proficient in one area are often assumed to be proficient in others.

Determining a Competency Level

It is the curiosity, risk-taking, relationship building, collaboration, teamwork and improved capabilities that have become the competitive weapons for the 21st century workplace. Through learning, education and experiences people develop the: (1) *Competency Skills*, which include intellect, expertise and characteristics that provide the ability to analyze and diagnose problems to determine the solutions; (2) *Human Skills*, the ability to understand, alter, lead and direct the actions of others; and (3) *Technical Skills*, the job significant awareness, expertise and technical savvy to be effective in identifiable work tasks.

The core competencies that structure a company's human capital will determine its market lead. All professions have their own array of competencies, making them exclusive, and although an individual's intellect and skills vary during their lifetime, their proficiency remains the same. To prosper, organizations should be interrelated and utilize the web of human capital, conduct and individual characteristics of their workforce. By directing its aim of competency, responsiveness, efficiency and innovative ability, an organization will undergo a measurable improvement in stimulating the highest ROI possible. It is estimated that labor costs range from 40 to 70 % of corporate expense, yet few companies make verdicts regarding their workers with the same discipline as with their other tangible assets. In order to measure the effectiveness of its human capital, organizations require a systematic list of the capabilities needed for its different processes. Since all intellect is the outcome of learning, management must examine the company's chronicle in determining its competency levels and the skills that have made it successful. Determining the levels through observation would be insufficient, as the process requires analyzing the relationships through activities in different scenarios, something not always possible through observation. No individual is exemplary in all competencies; and can improve in some way. With this inventory, management can assess each employee's intellect and skill level and determine what disparities exist and what must be done to close the gaps. Current market economics should provide a guide for what measured skills and knowledge may have to be recruited from outside of the organization.

Companies appear to have lost their true core focus. The appearance of diversifying in different areas is given in hopes of catching the brass ring, but they often find themselves in areas where they are often incapable of satisfying. For example, today's grocery stores have implemented so-called one-stop shopping by offering hardware, pharmaceutical products, lawn furniture, photo developing, flower shops, videotape rentals and even Christmas trees. Drug stores are similarly selling hardware, groceries, automotive parts, housewares, lawn furniture and other non-pharmaceutical products. In both examples, neither of the two provides value-added offerings driven by the corporate strategy. This diversity takes the store's focus from its true core competency, selling groceries or pharmaceutical products. Taking this line of attack frequently obscures a company's focus, which should be to satisfy its customer more fully.

The failed ventures of the 1970s and 1980s should have taught American business a lesson. Mergers and takeovers in trying to build empires that occurred in this period totaled a number greater than in all of history combined. At the same time, additional failures, service problems and quality issues were recorded as organizations were left with both a smaller number and inadequately trained staff. Companies have seemingly lost their entrepreneurial creativity and shrinking from competition, rivals are purchased in hopes of obtaining the competencies lacking allowing even more expansion. Any contemplating merging for the sake of creating a large-scale market should realize it might not be the best tactic.

Assessment Criteria

It is the judgment of those involved with an employee's work that makes the assessment process more meaningful. Employees should not be assessed on how intelligent they may appear, but to the dimensions of operation in relationship to one's job description, their role and provision of knowledge. When their work is assessed employees must be aligned with the process, and evaluated to defined effectiveness criteria rather than to the performance of others. Employees must be assessed to determine who has the *what* competencies, identified as critical to the organization. An assessment to prescribed performance effectiveness criterion based on attributes and how their tasks may be accomplished with an understanding of what they can contribute to the organization will require establishing criteria based on identified requirements. In addition, it is important to have a process in place to determine *how* to uncover and access the knowledge potential recruits may not know they have. Last of all, the process should measure and rank the intellectual worth of each individual and the organization combined. This will requirc measurements be in place to determine knowledge creation and improvements. To do so, measurements must be defined so the criteria determining the desired effectiveness is understood, qualified and quantified. Examples of employee performance should be defined to reflect the intellect levels desired and opportunities for the employees to think on their feet while exploring their strengths and weaknesses. Each employee should also be permitted to practice what they know, and be allowed to portion out their knowledge in order to make it easier to determine how they satisfy a particular task.

Human capital is an asset to be valued and an investment to be treated with dignity and admiration. Assessments performed correctly can be rewarding if they identify and characterize the competencies that may prove to be the prime source of an ability to effectively compete. Once an organization identifies its proficiency requirements it can determine its human capital. The Human Capital Evaluation Profile model in Figure 16 provides a method to assess employees based on the perceptions, observations and experiences found with fellow employees, subordinates, peers, supervisors, managers, suppliers and customers. This process may provide justification for investing in the workforce.

Each assessor should be able to place a merit on the knowledge and information sub-categories from their own analysis, and have an awareness and understanding of all processes driving the business, in addition to the competencies affected by the system. The number of assessors will vary based on the range of involvement by the assessed employee. Serving as an example to illustrate the criteria assessed, the performance criteria listed in the Human Capital Evaluation Model (Figure 17) are not exhaustive. The model serves as a guide to quantify the relevance of criteria. Following the elicitation of data the results obtained can be measured with a quantitative method to determine the ROI expected. Since intangibles represent a large portion of intellectual significance it is critical they are measured and valued for contributions to the organization. Following is one method that will help in determining meaning for the responses. What is critical is an understanding of the relationship of the many different characteristics and the nature in which they are involved, and by assigning values to each possible characteristic an individual's worth will increase as a person develops new potential.

Human Capital Evaluation Model

Process	Employee	Peer	Manager	Customer	Team Member	Supplier	
Dimensions of Performance	Evaluation Characteristic Value						Total
Knowledge							
Competencies							
Communications							
Behavior							
Attitude							
Performance							
Social Interaction							
Continuous Learning							
Innovative/Creative							
Internal Exchange							
Motivation							
Relevance							
Value of Responses							

Satisfaction Level →

Functional Excellence →

Figure 17

The evaluators involved in the process determine whether the employee can perform a particular task (Yes or No) or to some degree (Somewhat). A value can then be assigned to distinguish a high, average or low response, or using a Likert-type scale assigning a number (1-5) to the competencies identified as part of an individual's knowledge repository. Once determined, the scale value for each competency identifying a defined relationship can be maintained between the corporate strategic objectives and the employee's job description. In referencing the model, each of the *Dimensions of Performance* would have an assessment to determine a proficiency level for each scale. The number determined would then be multiplied by a dollar amount assigned to each dimension awarded based on defined importance. The totals will then identify a defined intellect level for each individual employee and the amount accumulated will determine the human capital significance for the organization plus its monetary value.

Evaluation processes must be collaborative and include self-assessments, those from supervisor(s), manager(s), peers in the workplace in addition to any customer(s) and supplier(s) with whom the assessed persons may interact. In a setting of trust and admiration the evaluation and assessment process can be an effective tool in the organization's tool kit and will be perceived by employees as a benefit, which will help management in determining cost effectiveness. It is management's responsibility for determining any imperative attributes dictated by the defined strategic initiatives. The findings from all of the assessors must be statistically analyzed using an analysis of variation. Averaging is straightforward, but the results must be analyzed for inconsistencies, and if any exist it is important to understand why.

Traditional organizations typically assess employees in helping to determine promotions, salary increases and downsizing efforts. The usual methods used nevertheless, are not affective when evaluating and validating their knowledge, and expertise. Any information and knowledge available may not be sufficient for proper and correct decision-making and the outcomes are often unfavorable. One possible outcome is that employees will become apprehensive when made aware of being accessed, evaluated or measured and consequently may react differently. They become *performers* in working to satisfy the process and not necessarily for improvement, and worry of reprisal if the requirements are met. To be successful with this process, new methods of managing human capital will be needed as current methods instill fear in the workforce, limiting the effectiveness of an assessment effort. To determine the effects desired employees must have a positive attitude, often the product of job satisfaction. Unfortunately, in the current work environment this may be difficult as a study by the Conference Board, determined that for the seventh consecutive year job satisfaction of U.S. workers aged 35 to 44 declined and continues to fall.

There are numerous characteristics that can distort the objectivity of an assessment process. Three key ones are a(n): (1) unconscious influence by one's emotions and bias; (2) belief that a particular slant is the only one, creating feelings of dissatisfaction; and (3) altering of the findings by inflating or deflating ratings in order to avoid conflict or to adhere to a bureaucratic deliberation. Training focus in the workplace has always been on *what workers need to, or should learn*, versus *what* is believed *needed to do* on the job. This action amounts to determining one's performance improvement needs and determining whether the outcomes produced effectively address the strategic initiatives. A development plan should include a needs analysis to reflect on the organization's essentials with the employee(s) realizing what new operations will be essential to perform or provide in the near term. Organizational and business benefits will be possible when an employee is successful in developing the new skills, intellect and expertise determined.

So-called expert judgment based on explicit performance criteria are difficult to measure, and not altering it in the process. As an example, the measurement process of communications involves the *sending* (verbal and non-verbal content) and *receiving* (state of mind of the receiver) aspects of information exchanged. This action forces the assessor to make decisions based on *what is sent* and *received,* something difficult when trying to determine the tone and feelings behind what is communicated. Ultimately this will require sensitivity in knowing and understanding the process from beginning to end and determining if there is a difference. From this interaction a determining reaction is made owing to a person's senses revolving around judgment, resulting in decisions based on the outcome of any contact. The end result will be either good or bad and one of three conclusions, *it is liked; not liked; or it is going to be ignored.*

The assessor is the first scientific tool in the measurement process, and all other resources involved are just extensions and it is vital that the assessor realize that desired or not the situation is constantly changing. This realization should provide freedom in establishing a person's likes or dislikes, but the tools used in the process must be capable of eliminating a possibility of bias. It is critical that the assessor is disciplined in determining acceptance or non-acceptance of a contributor's response. To do so legitimately will require that the assessor be involved and aware of a person's likes and dislikes while realizing their preferences. This involvement is imperative in order that the effects do not harm the assessor or the assessed individual contributors. Still, another problem is realizing that human capital judged to have meaning today may not have such in the future.

When researching and inquiring into assessments in hopes of determining if any might be available to weigh program successes, I determined that few models exist. As a result of the research, I concluded that to address the few models new interview guides, indicators questionnaires and surveys would have to be developed. Since the purpose of any assessment proposed should be to determine an organization's ability to adapt, it is important to insure that any assessment be consequential and informative. Ultimately, the closing stages of the assessment will identify particular human competencies and skills measured against the different standards associated through each assessment level and scope. The starting location must be to identify and determine how workers apply the know-how on hand, the frequency of the different uses of the knowledge, and all its sources that might contribute to the identifiable human capital determined. All of these efforts must be aligned to an organization's schemes. To accomplish this will require the right mix of intelligence and attitudes. In performing the assessment, the assessor will have to have an insight into the individuals, or they can be misled. Those interviewed often have a tendency to protect or promote themselves and inexperienced assessors may over emphasize some context, negatively overstating the information related.

Before assessments can be performed it is imperative that the assessors, process and the measurement tools used are calibrated. The relationship amid the two must be so infused that they can be removed from the aspects of either sending or receiving. By choosing to be involved, every employee must understand that they become an entity in the process and cannot be detached from the incident. Also having an understanding of the importance of synergism and involvement with the process is imperative and crucial that any problems involving the assessors and those being assessed be resolved. If assessment findings are ignored, discarded or interpreted incorrectly, and not reported properly, every person involved may be affected negatively. Assessments often promote a competitive atmosphere among personnel and when results denote a low rating in a given area the assessed individuals may develop a sense of fear, become defensive and or blame others for the situation.

What management and the employee desire and hope for is a realization of where and when some development help may be very important and if it was available. Another problem is when one employee's knowledge is compared to another. Any comparison may bring one's vanity into play, stimulating awkwardness and may even generate a feeling of or embarrassment for possible deficiencies. Assessment data is often misinterpreted because it is not always examined in the proper context. Many variables involved in the process, such as the diverse backgrounds and motivation levels of the workers, are seldom taken into account. It is essential therefore, that a strategic initiative is used to report assessment conclusions to those involved in the process. Fusing the assessment initiative with one or more others, all overlapping to help personnel will further develop their skills and generate greater acceptance of the process.

The Evaluation Process

Evaluations are used to interpret the information accrued from an assessment and making judgments and choices based on what has been determined and then placing a meaning to it. An effective evaluation process should include peers, subordinates, managers/supervisors, team members, customers and suppliers, using their insight, knowledge of requirements, and whatever is aligned to the strategic initiatives and experience to the particular characteristics assessed.

In a period requiring an understanding of how to evaluate the use of know-how as it corresponds to performance and productivity, little is known or understood on how the process should be performed. By tradition, the common practice is for a manager or supervisor to subjectively evaluate an employee's performance and intelligence. In today's setting of flat organizations a manager or supervisor may have too many direct reports to be able to objectively assess each individual with depth and honesty. It has been proven that ratings from peer, subordinates, team members, etc., can be more informative, in particular when done anonymously.

If done properly, evaluations are continually performed in an effort to accumulate the information needed to redirect efforts to plan for future development goals. One method might be workplace criterion referenced evaluations as determined by the human capital fundamental to addressing the strategic initiatives. Since no two workers perform the same work activity in the same manner or have the identical ability, the criteria used must reflect an employee's functioning based on identifiable work objectives.

In evaluating the exclusive criteria of an employee's activities it is essential to identify the more weighty aspects of the desired performance for the reason that there are numerous differences in the way practices are applied. These aspects must be described in terms that align the particular knowledge fundamental to promoting performance considering the possible numerous outcomes. It is essential that those involved in the evaluation understand, agree and adhere to the defined criteria and outcomes of the process. All selection techniques, interviews, tests, etc., must have acceptable levels of reliability and validity. The evaluators should be knowledgeable of the reviewed criteria and be able to categorize and describe the outcomes in a useful and concise manner. Examples of the precise operations desired and those acceptable must be included as something the individual contributors can compare against in performing the activities.

One is born with a natural inclination to learn. Learning is a source of innovation. One inherits a right to enjoy his work. Good management helps us to nurture and preserve these positive, innate attributes of people.

W. Edwards Deming

"The New Economy"

Chapter 9

Bringing it Together

It is apparent that in the present turbulent economy, organizational leadership must develop new ways and means to strengthen their business positions, and address the escalating challenges presented. One way that the challenges can be overcome in charting for future progress will be through more and expanded managing methods, and the leveraging of their most valuable and under-leveraged resource; the human capital in their organizations.

Human capital is not a structure of bricks and mortar, but one of men and women whose strength, creativity and innovative capabilities are found in their heads and those of their colleagues, peers, management, customers and suppliers. Understanding the organization's human capital is a facet of all jobs and the venue by which each employee works and applies awareness. The method of determining this valuable resource should be unique since it must not terrify and make people feel someone is looking to verify the unknown. From the assessment outcome, it is hoped workers will feel a need to build on what they are adequate at, and will continually work on building their strengths.

The atmosphere organizations must work to instill into their setting is a radical transformation somewhat difficult to describe and understand. It is an amoeba; made up of the products, services, people demographics and emergent change, and having the right people in the right place at the right time is central to the conversion.

The central focus of human capital is having access to the intellect of the workforce, whether located in the U.S., Latin America, Asia, Europe or anywhere else in the world. Success in the knowledge driven economy requires a shift in mind-set where greater receptiveness to ability is based on all workers working in cross-functional interactions to address real problems and issues. This can only occur in an environment where people collaborate, share experience, have common values and realize the significance of cognition to address problems.

Although still an emerging discipline, human capital extends into others such as: Organizational Excellence, Strategy, Operations Management, Marketing and Human Resources. This discipline emphasizes a formalized integrated slant to managing an organization's tangible and intangible assets. For most, vast amounts of human capital lie outside of the realm of other property (documents in file drawers, databases, e-mail messages and impromptu water cooler sessions). This categorization also includes the knowledge not in digital form, documented and or articulated *("the way we do things around here")* in an explicit *technique.* Regardless of where human capital originates, its meaning comes from the knowledge that creates or created the information used by the workforce. In summary, the human capital process is a coordinated effort that reaches out and captures concentrated consciousness in making more effective judgment.

Any priority placed on human capital will be subject to the particular business and culture, but to manage it will require nothing less than a radical conversion in thinking. A well-known proverb stating, "*You can't cross a chasm in two steps*," can refer to two steps of wisdom directed to people addressing the new global marketplace and the high running work setting. The steps involve people, and the method used to manage the knowledge learned will determine an organization's key strategic competitive advantage, because without workers it is impossible for companies to create new knowledge.

Organizational leaders are beginning to re-evaluate their ideas about human capital and are developing a strategic focus for its utilization. Realizing that their organizations are only using a fraction of their existing assets, management is beginning to develop new strategies to help in maximizing the use of this human capital. Nevertheless having the best strategies is not an end into itself; the right leaders are compulsory if the outcome desired is to be obtained. This will require leaders who can achieve a balance concerning the interests of the corporation, the workers and society as a group.

Shrinking Knowledge: Options and Alternatives

It has become fashionable for the media to report on business's turbulence coming into the 21st century. The business world is inundated with daily stories and events of unethical conduct and reminded of what management should and should not be doing as well as how companies should cope with these occurrences. With human capital continuing to grow in popularity the potential for stronger strategic alliances amid management, customers and suppliers increases in its importance and use. A problem confronted today is the manner in which management's values affect the organization. Society and management cannot look at current events and predict the future. To meet the variation, organizations must identify the root causes, and if necessary revert to a values-based organizational design. The product of change is a growing process that may necessitate relinquishing or modifying some habits. These habits, when interpreted and integrated with other learned knowledge can be recalled to strengthen the employee's ability and willingness to take on big challenges. All workers must feel they have ownership in the organization and are ready to address continuing trends and not just for the short-term. Ultimately, organizational transformation will occur and performance affected by accomplishing more than the Science of Management says is possible when organizations take care of the employee as a person, giving meaning and purpose to their lives.

Perception is reality evolving from the interpretation of the information presented to us, generating a thought process about the present activity bringing with it a series of associated events. In this way, if change is to be influenced, it will require changing the organization's belief systems; values, ideologies and thought processes. It must be realized that these belief systems may produce a different picture from the event as a result of the events and anxieties experienced. So how do organizations see their people? Are they perceived to be a drain; people who cannot be trusted or relied upon, requiring close control and monitoring or are looked upon as a valuable, resourceful asset, like a bee, pollinating knowledge throughout the organization.

Human capital management basically comes down to common sense and extending the Golden Rule of "*treating others as you would have them treat you*." The underlying reason for its limited implementation is that it appears to be a reflection on our current society rather than an absence of business skills. The human capital concept is truly the sharing of knowledge in order to expand an organization's innovative potential deterring decision-making and output. The real issue of contention is perhaps in its contribution to the bottom-line and not just added work.

Hours of Study (Effort)	Test Scores (Effect)
1	56
2	59
3	78
4	83

If management can understand the strength their employees have access to it is possible to make a difference in the shaping of an organization for the future. As the need for superior quality and customer dealings becomes more acute, it is apparent that if this energy were to be used correctly it would promote optimal solutions, as seen in the Table above. The improved results (effects) from additional hours of study (effort) can be seen in test scores as indicated.

To use workforce strength effectively requires something other than cosmetic change. Serious business changes involving an earnest obligation to a different manner of execution, etc. and a financial investment in resources (people, time, etc.) are required. There is a strong possibility management has reached the situation where they need to return to the paternal spirit promoted in the 1940's. The pendulum may have reached the position where it will return given that it can progress no further. It must now fall back as the importance of the community and concern in the workplace may once again have taken center stage. Management must redirect their *power from*, to one of *power to,* the ability to lead and work having people function collaboratively. The successful transition to the new 21st century economy of the Information Era is definitely calling for a return to *values-based-thinking*. It is a transition to the re-establishment of the paternalistic ways and ideals of Misters Ford, Watson, Reginald Jones, Hewlett and Packard and others, and not the promoters of a day's pay for a day's work theory. These individuals were typical of business leaders who inspired loyalty, encouraged moral integrity, celebrated innovation, who valued and respected their human assets, nurturing, mentoring and supporting them throughout their careers.

They were effective leaders who made a difference in the lives and organizations they touched through their Values-Based Management style. Values-Based Management begins with reverence, which has been proven to be a key motivator for employees, and the value that must pervade all aspects of the working environment. Employees want to be treated with respect and management must make certain that all communication and contact between them and the workers is governed by respect, ideas and values. Instilled ethical, moral values will influence how people act toward one another bringing definition to a common purpose, a commitment to strategy, dignity to human contact and an increased opportunity for growth and expression.

Developing a way of life-long learning and sharing is just a beginning. In all successful organizations people skills and the renewing of unique knowledge and expertise make the difference. It is the strength of a core competency developed as an upshot of realized learning that determines an individual's human capital worth. A company's human capital is usually under-utilized, with the implication that costs will be higher, productivity will be lower, and its competitive edge not as sharp. To remain competitive organizations must exploit their resources effectively. The human capital focus must be directed to the organizational environment, which holds the key to success. It is important to understand that a fundamental source of meaning lies in the capabilities supported by the human capital of the workforce. These resources are the hidden asset, which can be uncovered, constituting a virtual treasure chest for an organization. It is also the element people want management to know they possess, something that will give them greater stature in the workplace.

Human capital is a personal and human aspect that unless nurtured, encouraged and valued soon becomes dormant, stagnant and valueless. In reality the 21st century workplace is in the early stages of a transformation in knowledge and technologies challenging the way things are performed. To continue increasing productivity and minimize costs, modifications will have to be made in ways other than by means of layoffs and the transferring of work offshore. These methods have proven to fail and are believed to create greater harm than good, due to the mistrust, discontentment and little loyalty in the workplace. Traditional command-and-control management styles must be replaced by the use of core competencies, realized learning, individual steadfastness and collaborative efforts. Regardless of what one might hear, the current corporate interest in human capital cannot be a passing fad; it must be a strategic focus of improving how corporations come by, create, leverage and transfer knowledge and information.

Information systems must play a larger role in changing the organization's culture and help determine its structure and employee roles. This will require that the human capital process be assimilated into the operating locale or else it will fade into the sunset. The quantity and quality of human capital fosters enhanced execution, higher creativity and greater innovation.

Measures defined, developed and applied correctly become the critical activities in the process. It is essential to remember that assessments are data driven and subject to reliability (the consistency of the measure), validity (the measure of what it intends to measure) and repeatability (measuring the same unit using the same equipment).

Aligning organizational goals, performance objectives and the assessments to training make it easier to measure the effectiveness. Regardless of the strategy developed each person involved must realize cultural transformation is a long-term effort. In looking at a human capital strategy we see where it describes where an individual is, where they need to get to, and plans on how to get there. Just having knowledge does not imply the ideas have been internalized. It has taken years to develop the human capital in the workplace and a paradox can be found functioning on two different plains. The organization is static, functioning as it has for years on the first, while on the second they move at turbo speed by attempting to use the existing human capital to help build upwards from the foundation. The work situation is changing, functioning to a new set of rules, assumptions and insecurities, and creating an influence on the issue of human resources and values. The foundation of Maslow's[2] needs is affected, causing numerous problems with the work systems in place, which will require a re-organization to one that supports its values, ensuring advanced operation and greater wealth.

Companies are striving for competitive advantage and human capital is the most significant asset possible for innovation. Cognition may become the most critical asset needed to stay ahead of the competition and is made possible in the following ways; (1) knowing, having and being aware of the data or information essential to make knowledge driven decisions; (2) possessing the cognition required to make an improved decision; (3) shrinking the time to take action; (4) being proactive in implementing change; (5) anticipating problems and being more capable of responding to the unanticipated; (6) providing a steadfast, sustained marketplace advantage; and (7) helping in evaluating human tasks.

Many people are of the opinion that human capital

developed earlier is outdated and of little usefulness. Sharing managed learning, working in conjunction with the competencies of others, often becomes a primary resource by which a competitive advantage is based and the transferring of knowledge whether old or new, becomes a powerful tool and valuable, if it is still relevant. To help address the need for human capital, management must significantly improve their ability to understand their workforce, determine what is really important to them, regard their attained learning as a valuable, critical and ready to use resource. At the same time, it is vital these essential assets are acted upon before they are lost forever. To do so will require that organizations adopt a system which has a focus on its people, treating them as assets with value-added management capability and influence. People in turn, must work to develop and learn in order to provide the organization the knowledge mandatory in the future.

The American economy is in an era of transition, where the worker has been liberated and yet enslaved. They have been freed from manual labor requiring muscle and brawn to a background where one's human capital has become vital for all activities involved in the production of goods and services. A wide-ranging review of associated literature identifies no single tool to measure the many intangibles associated with one's knowledge level. Like all aspects discussed, the tools will require continuous innovation and change. This document concludes that regardless of the tool, it becomes a necessity to categorize the different elements involved before applying an evaluation process.

References

Introduction

1. Gibran, Kahlil, (1883 – 1931) was born in near Mount Lebanon. He was a poet, philosopher and artist. His best known book is the Prophet.

2. Watson, Thomas, Jr. (1962). *A Business and its Beliefs: The Ideas That Helped Build IBM.* New York, NY: McGraw-Hill Book Co. A collection of essays developed from a series of lectures he gave at Columbia University's Graduate School of Business.

3. Ringer Robert, (1995). *Looking Out for No. 1.* New York, NY: Fawcett Publications.

4. Brown, John Seely and Gray, Estee Solomon (1995). "The People are the Company," Fast Company. Boston, MA; Premier Issue, p.78-82.

5. Banks, H. W., (2000). *The First American: The Life and Times of Benjamin Franklin.* New York, NY: Doubleday.

6. Drucker, Peter F., (1989). *The New Realities.* New York, NY: HarperCollins Publishers.

7. Naisbitt, John, (1982). *Megatrends: Ten New Directions Transforming our Lives.* New York, NY: Warner Publishing.

Chapter 1

1. Thurow, Lester, C., (1996). *The Future of Capitalism.* New York, NY: William Morrow and Company.

2. Covey, Stephen, (1989). *The Seven Habits of Highly Effective People.* New York, NY: Simon & Schuster Inc.

3. Ryle, Gilbert (1949). *The Concept of Mind.* Chicago, Ill: The University of Chicago Press. An English philosopher who defined knowledge as *knowing how* and *knowing that* and that when we are thinking it is actually a manifestation of skill. His central concept was that as the human brain grows, it builds upon earlier, more

primitive brain structures.

4. Steier, David and Mitchell, Tom Michael, (1996). "Mind Matters." A Tribute to Allen Newell Published by Lawrence Erlbaum Associates, New York, NY.

5. Levitt, Theodore, (1991). *The Free Press*. Boston, Mass: Harvard Business School Press.

6. Roach, Stephen, (1998). "Manufacturing in Transition." Edited by Rich Delbridge and James Lowe. New York, NY: Routledge Publishing. p.115.

7. Morrow, L. (March 29). *The Temping of America*. Time, 1993.

8. Machlup, Fritz, (1984). *The Economics of Information and Human Capital* Princeton, NJ: Princeton University Press.

9. Drucker, Peter, F. (1993). *Post-Capitalist Society.* New York, NY: HarperCollins Publishers

10. Senge, Peter M., (1990). *The Fifth Discipline: The Art and Practice of the Learning Organization*, New York, NY: Doubleday.

11. Wheatley, Margaret, (1992). *Leadership and the New Science*. San Francisco, CA: Berrett-Koehler Publishers, Inc.

12. Zeleny, M., (1987). "Management Support Systems: Towards Integrated Knowledge Management." Human Systems Management, 7, 1, 59-70.

13. Kuan-Tse Huang, (1999). *Quality Information and Knowledge*. Upper Saddle River, NJ: Prentice Hall.

14. McGregor, Douglas, (2000). *Revisited: Managing the Human Side of the Enterprise*. New York, NY: John Wiley & Sons.

15. Deming, Edwards, W., (1986). *Out of the Crisis.* Cambridge, MA: MIT.

16. Senge, Peter M., (1990). *The Fifth Discipline: The Art and Practice of the Learning Organization*, New York, NY: Doubleday-Currency.

17. American Heritage Dictionary (1985). Boston, MA: Houghton Mifflin Company.

18. Garfield, Charles, (1987). writes "skills translate as competence, pride, confidence, and personal power, because they [workers] are motivated to use the skills to accomplish personally meaningful results." Avon Books. New York, NY. p. 116.

Chapter 2

1. Reich, Robert, (1991). *The Work of Nations.* New York, NY: Vintage Books.

2. Senge, Peter, (1990). *The Fifth Discipline: The Art & Practice of the Learning Organization.* New York, NY: Doubleday-Currency.

3. Sveiby, Karl-Erik, (1997). *The New Organisational Wealth – Managing and measuring Knowledge-Based Assets.* San Francisco, CA: Berrett-Koehler.

4. Belasco, James A., (1991). *Teaching the Elephant to Dance: The Manager's Guide to Empowering Change.* New York, NY: Penquin Group.

5. Drucker, Peter F. (1994). "The Age of Social Transformation." The Atlantic Monthly; November, Volume 274, No. 5; p. 53-80.

6. Polanyi, Michael (1967). *The Tacit Dimension.* London, UK: Routledge & K. Paul.

7. Nonaka, I. (1991). *The Knowledge Creating Company.* Boston, Mass: Harvard Business Review.

8. Deming, Edwards, W., (1986). *Out of the Crisis.* Cambridge, MA: MIT.

9. Mayo, Elton (1945). *The Social Problems of an Industrial Civilization.* Boston, Mass: Harvard University.

10. McCartin, Marybeth, Paula Feid (2001). "Information literacy for undergraduates: Where have we been and where are we going?" http://www.emeraldinsight.com/10.1016/S0065-2830(01)80018-0: Emerald Group Publishing Limited, Volume 25, pp. 1 – 27.

Chapter 3

1. Watson, Thomas John Sr. (1874–1956) was the president of International Business Machines (IBM), who oversaw that company's growth into an international force from the 1920s to the 1950s. Watson developed IBM's effective management style and turned it into one of the most effective selling organizations yet seen, based largely around a paternalistic approach, built around an almost religious set of beliefs..

2. Thomas Edison when interviewed by a young reporter who asked Mr. Edison if he felt like a failure and if he thought he should just give up by now. Perplexed, Edison replied, "Young man, why would I feel like a failure? And why would I ever give up? I now know definitively over 9,000 ways that an electric light bulb will not work. Success is almost in my grasp." And shortly after that, and over 10,000 attempts, Edison invented the light bulb.

3. Kanter, Rosabeth Moss (1989). *Where Giants Learn to Dance.* New York, NY: Simon & Schuster.

4. Brown, John, L, Moffett, Cerylle, (1999). *The Hero's Journey: How Educators Can Transform Schools and Improve Learning-*, Micklethwaite was quoted stating, "*A true learning organization is one in which knowledge ricochets around the system like a ball in a pinball machine.*"

5. The National Center on the Educational Quality of the Workforce (EQW), (1995). *The Other Shoe: Education's Contribution to the Productivity of Establishments.* Philadelphia, PA: University of Pennsylvania.

6. A study (1995) by the American Management Association (AMA) verified that 45% of the companies surveyed that invested in training after restructuring or down-sizing encountered productivity improvements, while over 42.8% of the companies that decreased their training budgets saw productivity decline and almost 30% realized lower profits.

7. Herman, Roger E. (1999). *Keeping Good people: Strategies for solving the #1 Problem Facing Business Today*. Fairfax, VA: Oakhill Press.

8. Zuboff, Shoshana, (1989). *In the Age of the Smart Machine*. Boston,

Mass: Butterworth-Heinemann.

9. Garvin, D. A. (July-August, 1993). "Building a Learning Organization." *Harvard Business Review* **71**, p.78-91.

Chapter 4

1. Einstein, Albert, Computers are incredibly fast, accurate, and stupid; humans are incredibly slow, inaccurate, and brilliant; together they are powerful beyond imagination.

2. Sejersted, Francis, September 29-30, 1997. Paper presented at the conference "The Impact of Information Technology on Society" organized by Bergen High-Technology Center.

3. Miyamoto Musashi. *The Five Rings: The Broad Principles of Musashi's Strategy*. its first English translation in 1974, Charles S. Terry (Translator)

4. Bernoulli, D. (c.1738) "Specimen Theorize Noval de Mensura Sortis (Exposition of a New Theory on the Measurement of Risk)." Translated from the Latin by Louise Sommer in Econometrica, 22 (1954): 23-26.

5. Thompson, A. A. Jr., Strickland, A. J. III, (1999). *Strategic Management*. Defined corporate culture as "*the way we do things around here*." Hightstown, NJ: McGraw-Hill Companies.

6. These findings concurred that the American Management Association (AMA) reported at least one-third (34%) of job applicants lacked the necessary skills to perform the jobs they sought.

7. Martin, L. (1991, July 26). Teaching tomorrow's skills. The Washington Post. Washington, DC. Samuelson, R. J. (1991, July 11). Gibberish on job skills. The Washington Post. Washington, DC. U.S. Department of Labor (1991). What work requires of schools: A SCANS report for America 2000. Washington, DC: The Secretary's Commission on Achieving Necessary Skills.

8. In 1991 SCANS issued its initial report as a five-year plan titled, *What Work Requires of Schools*. As outlined in the report "Learning a Living: A Blueprint for High Performance." a high performance workplace requires workers who have a solid foundation in the basic literacy and computational skills, in the

thinking skills necessary to put knowledge to work, and in the personal qualities that make workers dedicated and trustworthy.

9. Handy, Charles (1994). *The Age of Paradox*. Boston, Mass: Harvard Business School Press.

10. Miller. D. (1990). *The Icarus Paradox: How exceptional companies bring about their own downfall.* New York, NY: Harper Collins.

11. Now regarded as part of the Chaos Theory, Catastrophe Theory was developed in the late 1960s and presented quite independently by the mathematician René Thom in his book: "*Structural Stability and Morphogenesis*" (1994). Thom hoped to be able to predict the behavior of complex 'chaotic' systems. Boulder, CO: Westview Press.

Chapter 5

1. Shaw, George Bernard. "The Doctor's Dilemma." Release Date: February, 2004 [EBook #5070].

2. Einstein, Albert (2009). "The Quotations Page." Available: http://www.quotationspage.com/quote/23588.html

3. deGeus, Aries (1997). *The Living Company*, Springfield, Mo: Longview Publishing.

4. Peter Drucker on Asia (1997): A Dialogue between Peter Drucker and Isao Nakauchi. Butterworth-Heinemann. Linacre House, Jordan Hill, Oxford. p.105

5. Goethe, Johann Wolfgang von (1749-1832), German poet, dramatist, novelist, and scientist.

6. Friedman Thomas. In a February 12, 1997, *New York Times* article,

7. Ackoff, Russell, (2006). *The Little Book of F-Laws*. Axminister Ex13, UK: Triarchy Press. A collection of subversive epigrams.

8. Amidon, Debra (1997). *The Zen Awakening*. Boston, Mass: Butterworth-Heinemann.

9. Walton, Sam (1992). *Made in America.* New York, NY: DoubleDay.

10. Fredrick Winslow Taylor (1856-1915) is the author of Principles of Scientific Management American mechanical engineer who sought to improve industrial efficiency. He is regarded as the father of scientific management, and was one of the first management consultants.

11. Knonsuke Matsushita (1993). *Making Quality Work.* Harper Business, p37.

Chapter 6

1. Bridges, William (1994). *Jobshift: How to Prosper in a Workplace Without Jobs.* New York NY: Perseus Books.

2. Fredrick Winslow Taylor (1856-1915) is the author of Principles Of Scientific Management American mechanical engineer who sought to improve industrial efficiency. He is regarded as the father of scientific management, and was one of the first management consultants.

3. Deming, Edwards, W., (1986). *Out of the Crisis.* Cambridge, MA: MIT.

4. Chainsaw Al Dunlap – Business Week online : October 18, 1999 issue

5. Scott Adams, frustrated with the inanities of corporate America and its idiot bosses, created the comic strip "Dilbert" to lampoon all he considered repugnant-yet-funny in the workplace of cubicles. His title character Dilbert, the bespectacled MIT graduate with no mouth and flip-up tie, is part alter ego, part "every man." Dilbert was embraced by the comic-strip-reading public in 1989, and as of 2001, appeared through United Media's syndication efforts in an impressive 2,000 newspapers in 50-plus countries translated in 19 languages.

Chapter 7

1 Bacon, Sir Frances, (1561-1626). Argued that the only knowledge of importance to man was empirically rooted in the natural world;

and that a clear system of scientific inquiry would assure man's mastery over the world. He was the originator of the expression, "Knowledge is power."

1 Dixon, Nancy M. (1999). The Organizational Learning Cycle: How We Can Learn Collectively. Surrey, UK: Gower Publishing Ltd.

2 Kolb, D. (1984). *Experiential Learning: Experience as the Source of Learning and Development.* Englewood Cliffs, NJ: Prentice Hall.

3 Montague, William Pepperell (2005). *The Ways of Knowing or the Methods of Philosophy*. Whitefish, MT. Kessinger Publishing.

4 *Metcalf's Law and Legacy*, was first published in Forbes ASAP, September 13, 1993. It is a portion of George Gilder's book, Telecosm, published in 1996 by Simon & Schuster. Robert Metcalf's law states that the "*value*" or "*power*" of a network increases in proportion to the square of the number of nodes on the network. In other words, if you have four nodes, or computers, on a network, say, an office intranet, its "value" would be four squared (4^2), or 16.

5 Nonaka, I. (1995). *The Knowledge Creating Company*. New York, NY: Oxford University Press.

Chapter 8

1. Will Rogers. U.S. humorist & showman (1879 - 1935)

2. Drucker, Peter F., (1967). *The Effective Executive: The Definitive Guide.* Oxford OX2, UK: Butterworth-Heinemann.

3. ISR is an international employee research and consulting firm. Founded in 1974, ISR helps organizations to improve employee engagement, retain key talent, increase productivity, enhance customer satisfaction, and increase shareholder value. ISR has surveyed more than 35 million employees from more than 3,000 companies in 106 countries.

4. Reich, Robert, (1991). *The Work of Nations*. New York, NY: Vintage Books.

5. Kirkpatrick, Donald L., (1994). *Evaluating Training Programs:*

The Four Levels Second Edition. New York, NY: Berrett-Koehler Publishers.

6. Weiss, Alan (1995). *Our Emperors Have No Clothes: Incredibly Stupid Things Corporate Executives Have Done While Reengineering, Restructuring, Downsizing*. San Francisco, CA: Career Press.

Chapter 9

1. Deming, Edwards, W. (1986). *Out of the Crisis*. Cambridge, Mass: MIT.

2. Maslow, A. H., (1943). *A Theory of Human Motivation.* Originally Published in Psychological Review, 50, p. 370-396.

Subject Index

ABOUT THE AUTHOR

Dr. Polesky served over 40 years with Fortune 500 companies including General Electric, Honeywell, and IBM. Possessing an insatiable hunger for knowledge, he has earned a Doctorate in Organizational Development from the Union University and Institute in Cincinnati, Ohio, and a Masters degree in Business/quality from the University of Miami in Coral Gables. He completed his undergraduate degree at Grand Canyon University, Phoenix, Arizona.

His extensive education and work experience have inspired his capturing the imagination of academic, government and industrial leaders around the globe. He is recognized as a management and leadership innovator and has taught Leadership and Management courses in universities throughout North and South America, as well as Europe. He also developed an undergraduate curriculum for the Twenty-First Century workplace which has been incorporated into several American college and university offerings.

During his tenure with General Electric he was involved with designing and developing several management training courses for the company's Corporate University at Crotonville, NY, and was deeply involved with the company's implementation of Lean Six Sigma where was certified as a Master Black Belt. An author of several seminal publications, he contributed to the *Collaborative Innovation and the Knowledge Economy* practices handbooks for The Society of Management Accountants of Canada.